Uncle John's
BATHROOM
READER®

Book of
L·O·V·E

Uncle John's
BATHROOM
READER®

Book of L·O·V·E

PORTABLE
PRESS

Bathroom Readers' Institute
San Diego, California, and Ashland, Oregon

Uncle John's Bathroom Reader
Book of Love

For information, write
Bathroom Readers' Institute,
5880 Oberlin Drive, San Diego, CA 92121
e-mail: unclejohn@advmkt.com

Library of Congress Cataloging-in-Publication Data
Uncle John's bathroom reader book of love.
p. cm.
ISBN-13: 978-1-59223-742-5
ISBN-10: 1-59223-742-8
1. Love--Humor. 2. Love--Miscellanea. I. Bathroom Readers'
Hysterical Society (San Diego, Calif.)
PN6231.L6U63 2007
818'.00803543--dc22

2006022875

Printed in Canada
First printing: November 2006
Second printing: January 2007

07 08 09 10 11 6 5 4 3 2

Contents

In Holy Matrimony

Rings 'n' Things

Places to Go

Mixed Bag

Quizzes and Puzzles

The truth [is] that there is only one terminal dignity—
love. And the story of a love is not important—what is
important is that one is capable of love. It is perhaps
the only glimpse we are permitted of eternity.

—*Helen Hayes*

Project Team

Gordon Javna, Editor-in-Chief
JoAnn Padgett, Director, Editorial and Production
Melinda Allman, Developmental Editor
Jennifer Payne, Production Editor
Jennifer Thornton, Managing Editor
Connie Vazquez, Product Manager

Thank You!

The Bathroom Readers' Institute sincerely
thanks the following additional people whose advice
and assistance made this book possible.

Julia Papps
Michael Brunsfeld
Kirk Henderson
Sydney Stanley
Rebecca Kaiser
Friesens
Dan Mansfield
Amy Miller
Barb Porsche
Matthew Shores
Kim K.

Hysterical Scholars

The Bathroom Readers' Institute sincerely thanks the following talented people who contributed selections to this work.

Toney Allman
Jane Louise Boursaw
Myles Callum
J. Carroll
Jenness I. Crawford
Jacqueline Damian
Christina Factor
Debbie K. Hardin
Kerry Kern
Megan Kern
Andy Levy-Ajzenkopf
Lea Markson
Ryan Murphy
Stephanie Spadaccini
Lori Hall Steele
Rachel Steiner
Susan Steiner

Introduction

Here at the Bathroom Readers' Institute, love is always in the air. Whether it's Valentine's Day, Flag Day, or just Wednesday, we're always celebrating that little thing called love.

And because we know our readers are as sentimental as we are, we decided to share the love. We're here to tell you . . .

- For whom the song "Unchained Melody" was written.
- How hippos, honeybees, and bowerbirds express their love.
- The cost of an average American wedding.
- Why brides stand on the left and grooms on the right.

And that's just the beginning. As we delved into a treasure trove of love stories, we also asked a lot of questions.

- What romantic movie included the first kiss? The first interracial kiss? The first French kiss?
- Who declared lipstick fit only for actors and prostitutes?
- Just how long did the world's longest kiss last?

- How can you use pheromones to pick a mate?
- What flower asks someone to dance? Professes love at first sight?
- How many women did Casanova sleep with, anyway?
- Who invented greeting cards?
- Did a collection of love letters bring down Mary, Queen of Scots?
- Where did the term "honeymoon" come from?

So, cuddle up with your beloved to share sweet nothings. We hope you enjoy this collection—our love letter to you.

As always, go with the flow . . .

Valentine Queen

In photographs, she presents the grim, humorless visage
of a middle-aged, Victorian spinster. But Esther Howland
popularized valentine giving in the United States and, by
the time of her death in 1904, had earned the sobriquet
"Mother of the American Valentine."

Be My Valentine?

Esther was born in 1828 in Worcester, Massachusetts, the daughter of a successful businessman, Samuel E. Howland, who owned a book and stationery store. When Esther graduated from Mount Holyoke College in 1847, one of her father's business acquaintances mailed her a valentine from England. Such greeting cards were popular in Europe, where they were mass-produced. But Americans, having no such products available, usually made their own simple greeting cards because the imported English cards were expensive. Charmed by the concoction of paper lace and cutout flowers, Esther decided to try to imitate it.

She asked her father to buy lace, colored paper, and other trimmings and then proceeded to design 10 different valentines with her supplies. When she finished, she asked one of her salesman brothers to show her designs to his business contacts throughout New England. She hoped to sell her valentines for 50 cents each and earn a few hundred dollars. Her brother returned with requests for 10,000 cards—an order that amounted to $5,000!

A Lovely Business

Unable to produce so many valentines by herself, Esther took over a room in her family's home and persuaded some of her friends to help her. Together, they created one of the first (though unofficial) assembly lines in the United States: One woman made the backgrounds— fancy curlicues, leaves, or landscapes. A second cut out pictures to be layered on lace paper. A third pasted on flowers or bits of silk and satin. Esther examined and approved every card.

Those 10,000 cards were just the beginning. Esther fulfilled her initial orders by 1849, and by the end of the next year, the amount had doubled. Her business took

over the whole third floor of her father's home and then required even more space. So, in the 1860s, Esther rented a nearby building to house her operation and named her business the New England Valentine Company. She was also making about $100,000 per year.

For the next 20 years, she continued to create the

2

cards. She had designs to fit every pocketbook. The cheapest and most simple were usually two-dimensional and sold for 5 cents. But the most complex (valentines with lift-up windows, 3-D shadow-box scenes, and pleated layers) could cost as much as $50. She used crushed colored glass to create a sparkling effect and even made cards with tiny envelopes in which the giver could hide sweet sentiments for his beloved. Esther also published a book of valentine "mottoes," or verses, so that senders could choose their own messages.

In 1881, Esther retired and sold her business. The buyer, George Whitney, had a large card company of his own and was one of the first to manufacture card-making supplies in the United States. But by that time, Esther had transformed valentine giving from a luxury of the upper classes to something everyone could do.

Endless Love

The cards Esther made are sought-after collectibles today. They are hard to find, though, and the most elaborate ones can cost several hundred dollars. Some identifying marks reflecting different periods in her business include a red "H" sticker, a printed red "H," or an embossed "NEV Co." (for New England Valentine Company). The Mount Holyoke College Archives and Special Collections owns two original Howland valentines. And the Elmhurst Historical Museum in Illinois boasts a large valentine archive that includes Esther Howland cards.

To recognize Esther's contributions to the Valentine's Day card, the Greeting Card Association (the international organization of greeting card and stationery publishers) established the Esther Howland Award in 2001. Each year, this award goes to an individual whom the association recognizes as a creative visionary in the industry. The first recipient was Marian Heath, aged 95, who established Marian Heath Greeting Cards during the 1940s. The company is still in business.

Hey, Lover Boy . . .

Not everyone in Esther Howland's day appreciated sweet, lover-ly valentines. For some, flowery sentiments were more than they could stomach. These folks came up with the "penny dreadful" or "vinegar valentine." A cheap, insulting card first introduced in 1858, vinegar valentines cost one cent and were usually sent anonymously. What might one say? Things like . . .

- "Hey, Lover Boy, the place for you is home upon the shelf, 'cause the only one who'd kiss you is . . . a jackass like yourself!"
- "You're a grafter, a grabber and bully, the biggest one in all the town, but when it comes to school work—you are a dunce of great renown."
- "You try to do all that is the rage, although you're fat and carry weight for age. If you would do as we advise, you'd act more consistently with your size."

A Rite of Passage: Then and Now

Proms (short for "promenade," a 19th-century ball) began in the 1920s as small, formal events where young people could learn and practice proper social behavior. My, how times have changed.

1920s

Attire: Their Sunday best.

Music: Recorded music (without DJs) and sometimes live orchestras were the norm.

Flowers: Exchanging flowers wasn't part of the mix at early proms; the practice started to become fashionable during the early 1960s.

Transportation: Mom and Dad

21st century

Attire: Girls buy dresses, shoes, and accessories, and guys rent tuxedos. Spending averages from $300 to $500 per student.

Music: DJs and live bands are popular.

Flowers: Some wear corsages and boutonnieres, but exchanging flowers is less popular today than it was just 10 years ago.

Transportation: Many attendees rent limousines, which

can cost between $100 and $150 per hour, with a three-hour minimum. Often, several couples share the ride to make this option a little more inexpensive.

You Say "Prom," We Say . . .

Dances at the end of the school year are popular throughout the Western world. Britain also calls such dances "proms." But Australia and New Zealand label them "formals" or, if there's a meal involved, "leavers dinners" (the graduates are called "leavers"). And in Ireland, the dance is known as a "debs," short for "debutante ball."

A Work of Art

This guy knows that the way to a woman's heart is through . . . a piece of art?

Charlie wanted to find a unique way to propose to his girlfriend Kelly, so he taped a diamond ring to his chest and used the x-ray machine at his office—he's a doctor, after all—to take a photo of the ring above his heart. Then he called in a favor and had the photo included in an art exhibit he knew Kelly would attend. It wasn't long before Kelly and her friend visited the gallery and noted the photo, entitled "I Love You Endlessly." The subtitle was "Kelly, Will you marry me?" and the artist, of course, was "Charlie." (She said yes.)

Valentine's Day
By the Numbers

The roses . . . the chocolates . . . the cards!
Take a look at the numbers.

15 percent
Number of American women who send themselves flowers on Valentine's Day

50
Times more often Internet searches record "gifts for him" than "gifts for her"

$77.43
Average amount consumers spend on Valentine's Day gifts; the three most popular gifts are candy, flowers (roses, in particular), and stuffed toys.

1,000+
Letters that arrive in Verona, Italy, every Valentine's Day addressed simply to "Juliet," presumably of William Shakespeare's *Romeo and Juliet*.

1,330

Number of different Hallmark Valentine's Day cards on sale each year

3,523

Stores in the United States that specialize in selling candy—for buying those chocolate hearts

130 million

Roses sold nationwide between February 12 and February 14, 2002

180 million

Valentine's Day cards exchanged every year among adults in the United States. Children exchange another 65 million valentines with teachers, friends, and parents. And Valentine's Day is the second-most popular card-giving holiday in the United States (Christmas is first).

Did You Know?

The 1957 film *Island in the Sun* featured the first interracial on-screen romantic kiss. The lovers: Joan Fontaine and Harry Belafonte.

The Bigger the Better, Part 1

Not only size (or carat weight) but also cut, clarity, and color matter when it comes to evaluating a diamond's quality. Here's a brief rundown of some of the most impressive and famous diamonds of all.

Biggest Celebrity Stone

Elizabeth Taylor received many lavish gifts of jewelry from her fifth (and sixth) husband, actor Richard Burton. But the most extravagant was the 69-carat pear-shaped stone he gave her for her 40th birthday, a jewel that came to be known as the "Burton-Taylor Diamond." The stone was the centerpiece of a necklace (studded with many other multicarat diamonds), and it required its own security force to transport it from event to event.

But diamonds were not forever with Taylor. In 1978, after her second divorce from Burton, she sold the necklace for more than $5 million. Taylor used the proceeds to build a hospital in Botswana, Africa.

Biggest Diamond Mined

The largest diamond ever mined is the "Cullinan," which originally weighed 3,106 carats. Miners in Gauteng, South

Africa, found the stone in 1905. It was eventually cut into three parts and then subdivided into 11 gem-quality stones. The biggest of these, "Cullinan I" (later renamed the "Great Star of Africa"), is a pear-shaped beauty that tops the scales at 530 carats. It reigned for many years as the largest polished diamond in the world. "Cullinan II," called the "Lesser Star of Africa," weighs 314 carats and is the third-largest polished diamond in the world. It's currently part of the British Crown Jewels and is on display at the Tower of London.

Biggest Polished Diamond

First dubbed the "Unnamed Brown," this unattractive-sounding beige diamond was found in 1985 in South Africa. When cutter Gabi Tolkowsky polished and cut it, the diamond was transformed from an ugly brown duckling to a dazzling golden swan. It weighs almost 546 carats, making it the largest polished diamond in the world. It has since been renamed the "Golden Jubilee," and it now belongs to Thailand's King Rama IX, who mounted the stone in his scepter.

Most Colorful

Five stones vie for the title of most colorful:

1. The "Dresden Green Diamond," a 41-carat natural green diamond, dates to the early 18th century and is such a deep green that it actually looks like an emerald. The unusual natural tint is attributed to radioactive materials that were present where the diamond was mined.

2. The "Moussaieff Red Diamond," a triangular cut stone measuring a little more than five carats, is the world's largest red diamond.

3. "Heart of Eternity" is unique because it's a deep blue, nearly 28 carats, and its cut is unusual: it's shaped like a heart, a cut that requires a large diamond. Gems like this one generally sell for $550,000 to $580,000 per carat.

4. As the name suggests, the "Pumpkin Diamond" is orange; it was discovered in 1997 in South Africa. The House of Harry Winston (jeweler to the rich and famous) currently owns the gem, which is valued at $3 million.

5. The "Black Orloff" diamond, discovered in India in the early 19th century, was part of a larger diamond that originally weighed 195 carats. According to legend, a monk stole that raw diamond—supposedly, he pulled it from the eye of a statue of the Indian deity Brahma. Because of this, many people worried that the stone was cursed. In an effort to break the curse, the diamond was cut into three different stones. The largest one is the Black Orloff, which weighs $67\frac{1}{2}$ carats. The diamond's black color comes from magnetite and hematite minerals in the stone.

To read about more famous diamonds, turn to page 69.

Strange Bedfellows

Colonial Americans who wanted to find a mate sometimes relied on a curious practice called bundling.

Bundle Up

Bundling originated in Britain and the Netherlands and came to colonial America with the Pennsylvania Dutch. It consisted of a young, unmarried couple spending the night together in the same bed. The pair remained fully clothed, and the practice was both sanctioned and facilitated by the young woman's family.

When a colonial man went courting, he visited a young woman's home in the evening after his own chores were finished. Rather than go home in the dark, he spent the night with his beloved. In this way, the young couple

could talk late into the night and get to know one another. Sometimes the man and woman were separated by a wooden partition, known as a "bundling board," that divided the bed. Other times, they were sewn into specially made sacks or tied to the bedding to prevent any funny business.

Hey, Baby

Those preventive measures didn't always work, and many women got pregnant before they were married. Surprisingly, the community was pretty forgiving of these indiscretions. As long as the couple got married (which nearly all of them did), the pregnancy wasn't a cause for concern.

Bundling began to wane during the 19th century when lawmakers and religious leaders became increasingly concerned about the morality of the practice. By the 20th century, it had all but vanished from American culture, though some Amish communities still use bundling today.

Nice Day for a White Wedding?

Wedding dresses weren't always white. Throughout history, most women got married in whatever dress they had available, no matter the color. But in 1840, England's Queen Victoria married Prince Albert, and she wore a white gown. Although Victoria wasn't the first royal to wear a white dress, she was the first whose wedding photos were widely published. Suddenly, women all over England wanted to emulate the queen. Those who had the money chose elaborate white dresses for their weddings, and soon, wearing white at a wedding became associated with wealth and status (which made it popular among the rich and desirable for common folk).

Prime Time Dating

Dating, reality TV–style: here are some of the most popular reality dating shows to make their way onto television in recent years.

Who Wants to Marry a Multi-Millionaire?

Premiered: February 15, 2000

Peak number of viewers: 22.8 million

Before the new millennium, most TV dating shows, like *The Dating Game*, consisted of a contestant choosing one of three singles with whom to (hopefully) enjoy a romantic encounter paid for by the series. But in 2000, a single episode of *Who Wants to Marry a Multi-Millionaire?* changed all that:

1) The show enticed potential brides with the prospect of financial gain.
2) The bachelor—Rick Rockwell, an investor and comedian—evaluated 50 suitors.
3) The bachelor was to marry the winner live on TV, even though the two had never met (Rockwell observed the contestants as they performed onstage).

The women modeled swimwear and wedding dresses in an effort to get Rockwell's attention, and in the end, he chose war-veteran-turned-emergency-nurse Darva Conger as his quickie bride. The couple then embarked on a honeymoon on the show's tab.

Reality was not rosy, however. On the honeymoon, Rockwell and Conger did not get along, and the marriage was quickly annulled. The media also discovered that the groom had been accused of manhandling an ex-fiancée who had been granted a restraining order against him.

The show didn't last either. The Rockwell/Conger episode was the only one that ever aired. But *Who Wants to Marry a Multi-Millionaire?* and its high ratings inspired a slew of similar programs.

The Bachelor and The Bachelorette

Premiered: March 25, 2002 *(The Bachelor)*; January 8, 2003 *(The Bachelorette)*
Peak number of viewers: 18.5 million *(The Bachelor)*; 17.6 million *(The Bachelorette)*

The Bachelor and *The Bachelorette* feature one romantic hopeful who spends a season dating 25 singles. Some moments are happy as the star and suitors share horse-drawn carriage rides and other dates. But heartbreak abounds as the bachelor or bachelorette weeds through the suitors, and each episode ends with the elimination of would-be soul mates. The suitors also live together and vie for the bachelor or bachelorette's attention on group dates (leading to arguments, jealousy, and high ratings). By the season's end, the star has usually "fallen" for one or more companions, gone on intimate overnight dates with them, met their families, and shopped with them for just-in-case engagement rings. In the last episode, the finalists dress in their finest and wait to be either embraced or dumped.

Although most of the winning couples have split, *The Bachelor/Bachelorette* franchise has produced dating TV's only successful marriage to date. Trista Rehn, who was rejected on *The Bachelor*'s first season, got a second chance for love in season one of *The Bachelorette*. In the finale, she became engaged to Ryan Sutter, a fireman and part-time model. In December 2003, a TV special chronicled their $3.7 million wedding.

Turn to page 59 for more prime time dating.

Bad Dates: My Dream Guy

"After meeting a man through a popular Internet dating site, I decided to meet him for a drink at a local watering hole. He was cute, polite, and seemed OK. The conversation wasn't stimulating, but I didn't feel like I was suffering. Well, I had a vodka and tonic and he had a Long Island—scratch that, four Long Islands! After the second drink, he confessed that he had lied about his job and was really an out-of-work actor. Great! An actor with no work, my dream guy. As the Long Islands were poured, this guy proceeded to get drunk. Eventually, he passed out on the bar. I put a round of drinks for strangers on his tab, told the bartender to find him a cab, and left him drunk on the bar."

—*Kim K.*

Flower Power

Red roses symbolize love and desire. But there are flowers for every occasion. This list will help ensure you pick the flower that says just what you mean.

Camellia (pink)	"I'm longing for you."
Carnation (yellow)	"You have disappointed me."
Daffodil	"You are the only one."
Dogwood	"My love is undiminished by adversity."
Gloxinia	"Love at first sight."
Hyacinth (purple)	"Please forgive me."
Lily (yellow)	"I'm walking on air."
Lily of the valley	"You've made my life complete."
Petunia	"Your presence soothes me."
Spider flower	"Elope with me."
Sweet pea	"Sorry I can't be with you. Good-bye."
Tulip (yellow)	"There is sunshine in your smile."
Viscaria	"Will you dance with me?"

Wedding Traditions

*Throw rice, share a wedding kiss, carry the bride
over the threshold—you know the traditions,
but do you know how they began?*

Bridal Veil

Veils protected brides from external forces meant to taint
them (other men, prurient influences, etc.). When the
groom lifted the veil during the wedding ceremony, he was
showing that he would now protect her.

Wedding Kiss

This has at least two symbolic meanings:

1. In ancient times, a kiss was a legally binding way to seal
   a contract. Brides and grooms who kissed after the ceremony were sealing the deal.
2. It's also a throwback to the days when couples were
   required to consummate their marriage in the presence
   of several witnesses, to ensure that the consummation
   actually took place.

Bride's Garter

The tradition of throwing the bride's garter comes from a
rowdy practice in which groomsmen fought each other to
see who would get it (the garter was supposed to bring

good luck to the person who possessed it). But the Catholic Church frowned on such riotous activity, so it was eventually replaced by a milder custom: the groom tossing the garter to his groomsmen.

Bride on the Left/Groom on the Right

Today, weddings are usually well-planned and sedate affairs, but a thousand years ago, they could be raucous. Bandits or raiding parties would often crash weddings to kidnap or free (depending on the circumstances) the bride. A groom always had to have his right hand free to draw his sword to fend off such an attack, and because his bride was on his left side (typically putting him between her and the wedding crashers), he was well situated to defend her from the attack.

Throwing Rice

Throwing rice has several explanations; here are two:
1. It was used as a symbol of fertility; guests threw rice at the bride in the hope that she'd bear children the way wheat produced bread.
2. It also was a way for guests to wish the married couple prosperity and a life of plenty; they threw rice as a way to say, "We hope you always have a full pantry."

June Weddings

It was customary for Romans to marry in June to honor the queen of the gods, Juno, who was also the goddess of women. They hoped to win her favor to make the marriage last and to make childbirth easier.

Carrying the Bride Over the Threshold

Ancient Romans thought good and evil spirits hung around the entrance of a home. They also believed that if you walked into your house left foot first, the evil spirits won. So to be sure the bride—whom Romans figured was "in a highly emotional state and very apt to be careless"— didn't accidentally step into her new home with the wrong foot, the groom picked her up and carried her.

Wedding Cake

In one form or another, wedding cakes have been around since the days of the Roman Empire, when an attendant would crumble a thin wheat loaf over the bride's head to encourage fertility. Guests picked up and ate the crumbs as

 good-luck charms. During medieval times, guests began bringing small "bride-cakes" to just-married women (still to encourage fertility); those cakes were stacked high, and the bride and groom kissed over the pile for good luck. Finally, bakers began covering the stacked cakes with frosting and serving them to the guests.

The Bridal Chorus

Composer Richard Wagner created "Bridal Chorus" in 1848 for his opera *Lohengrin*. The song played during a racy scene in which the story's newly married Princess Elsa joins her groom in the bridal chamber for the first time. Ten years later, Queen Victoria's daughter Princess Vicky, who admired Wagner's work, used "Bridal Chorus" during her entrance at her January 25, 1858, wedding to Friedrich Wilhelm of Prussia. Succeeding brides followed in Vicky's royal footsteps.

Please, Please, Marry Me!

Darren wanted desperately to marry his girlfriend, Annette. He left love notes all over their house asking her to tie the knot. He sent her text messages. In all, he proposed 85 times. But Annette always said no; previous relationships had left her wary, and even though she loved Darren, she wasn't sure that marriage was right for them. But in 2003, after being diagnosed with cancer, Annette changed her mind. Darren supported her through her operation and took care of her in the months afterward. So she decided to surprise him with a wedding and concocted a story about attending a cousin's nuptials. When she and Darren arrived at the church, she greeted him with a rousing "Will you marry me?" He, of course, said yes.

She Said

Aw, ladies . . . you're such romantics. Can you match these quotes to the famous women who said them?

A. Madonna
B. Pearl Bailey
C. Agatha Christie
D. Helen Keller
E. Mae West

F. Lily Tomlin
G. Isadora Duncan
H. Edith Head
I. Rita Rudner
J. Katharine Hepburn

1. "Your clothes should be tight enough to show you're a woman and loose enough to show you're a lady."
Hint: Costumer to the stars

2. "What the world really needs is more love and less paperwork."
Hint: American Broadway star

3. "Art is not necessary at all. All that is necessary to make this world a better place to live in is to love."
Hint: Martha Graham, eat your heart out!

4. "If love is the answer . . . please rephrase the question?"
Hint: Laugh-In made her famous.

5. "A man in love is like a clipped coupon—it's time to cash in."
Hint: Her middle name was really Jane, but some say it ought to have been "Bawdy."

6. "Before I met my husband, I'd never fallen in love, though I'd stepped in it a few times."
Hint: American comedian and writer

7. "An archaeologist is the best husband any woman can have; the older she gets, the more interested he is in her."
Hint: World's best-known mystery writer

8. "Love has nothing to do with what you are expecting to get—only with what you are expecting to give—which is everything."
Hint: Witty star of stage, film, and television

9. "To be brave is to love someone unconditionally, without expecting anything in return."
Hint: A material girl

10. "Love is like a beautiful flower which I may not touch, but whose fragrance makes the garden a place of delight just the same."
Hint: Extraordinary American lecturer, author, and activist

To read what the men have to say, turn to page 156.
For answers, turn to page 172.

♡

Scratch and Sniff

Throw away those personal ads. Cancel your online dating service. You've already got what it takes to find a mate. Just take a deep breath—through your nose.

The Power of Pheromones

Scientists first stumbled onto nose power when they studied pheromones in animals and insects. The word *pheromone* comes from the Greek words *phero*, "I carry," and *hormone*, "to excite." So the word literally means "I carry excitement." And they do. Pheromones are chemicals that send signals between members of the same species. In animals and insects, pheromones can command sexual arousal or sexual receptivity. Humans have more of a choice—or at least they think they do.

Pheromones are supposedly odorless, but mammals detect them with an organ inside the nose—called the vomeronasal organ (VNO)—a pair of microscopic pits on the skin inside the nostrils. When the VNO picks up a chemical order from pheromones, get out of the way!

Animal Love

Here are some findings from the animal kingdom:

- Male mice emit pheromones so potent they actually promote the sexual development of nearby female mice.

- A male moth can detect the pheromones of a female moth from more than a mile away and has no choice but to fly toward her.
- Male cockroaches may be the most pheromone-crazy creatures of all. When a glass rod is doused with female cockroach pheromones, the males try to mate with the rod.

Guys in Sweaty T-shirts

But how does all this apply to us? Human love is deep and spiritual—right? Skeptics claim that the VNO isn't functional in adult humans; it can't possibly react to pheromones. Here's what the research showed:

- Underarm sweat has a pheromone component produced by the chemical androstenol. An experiment showed that exposure to androstenol made females more inclined to have social interactions with males (easy, boys, that's *social* interactions).
- When women were asked to smell unwashed T-shirts worn by different men, they liked the smell of men whose immune systems were different from their own. Since different genes emit different smells, the women may have been sniffing for an evolutionary advantage— a combination of immune-system genes that would be better at fighting off infections.
- Extracts of skin cells with pheromones contained in open flasks made people (male and female) warmer and friendlier. When the flasks were closed, the camaraderie faded.

- Pheromone-laced perfume increased women's sexual attractiveness. Women got more requests for dates and sexual intimacy.
- A set of female twins—one doused with pheromones, the other with witch hazel—secretly traded places at a singles' bar. The one wearing the pheromones was approached nearly three times as often as her witch hazel–wearing sister.
- Men "under the influence" of pheromones found plain women more attractive—and beautiful women less so.

Stop Paying Through the Nose

There are lots of pheromone products on the market, but are they really the love potions they purport to be? Scientists aren't sure. One thing they agree on is that the nose plays an important part in mating. People who are born blind or deaf engage in normal sexual behavior, but people born with no sense of smell tend to have diminished sexual behavior.

The Turn-ons and Turnoffs

In more research, it was found that men were most aroused when they caught a whiff of lavender combined with pumpkin pie. Women went wild over licorice and cucumber. Women were definitely turned off by the scent of cherries and barbecue smoke. What smells turned men off? Well, none, actually. It seems it's pretty tough to discourage a guy who's got love on the brain. Or is it on the nose?

Seven Things You Don't Know About Casanova

More than 200 years after his death, Giacomo Girolamo Casanova remains Europe's most legendary lothario. And even though his reputation for debauchery is well documented, the truth of his exploits and of his personal life are not.

1. He didn't have *that* many conquests.

Modern ladies' man Wilt Chamberlain claims to have had affairs with 20,000 women; by comparison, Casanova said he slept with (only) 122.

2. He was successful with women because he actually liked them.

Casanova was unique for his time. He enjoyed female companionship, lavished praise on women, loved listening to them talk, and was an attentive lover. He also remained friends with many of the women he romanced long after the affairs were over.

3. He got dumped.

Casanova nearly settled down when he met a young French woman named Henriette in Cesena, Italy. She was masquerading as a male opera singer, a ruse she created to escape an unwanted marriage proposal. But her disguise didn't fool Casanova, and the pair struck up a relationship. Henriette and Casanova were an item from July 1749 until February 1750, but Henriette ultimately broke off their affair and left Casanova to return to her family. The pair reconnected in 1769 through letters, but they never saw each other again. The loss of Henriette was devastating for Casanova.

4. He was a romantic.

According to Casanova, "Real love is the love that sometimes arises after sensual pleasure: if it does, it is immortal; the other kind inevitably goes stale, for it lies in mere fantasy."

5. He introduced the lottery to France.

Women weren't Casanova's only entertainment; he also liked to gamble at Europe's many casinos. In the 1750s, he decided to bring gambling to Paris, his adopted hometown. An old friend and an influential French cardinal named Abbe de Bernis introduced Casanova to France's King Louis XV, with whom he shared his idea of creating a simple state lottery. Louis loved the idea, and the first lottery began in Paris in 1757.

6. He used lemons as contraceptives.

Casanova used empty half-rinds of lemons as cervical caps. The lemon's chemical properties (particularly its high acidity) also worked as a spermicide and even combated some sexually transmitted diseases. Although Casanova didn't invent this technique, he did make it part of his daily life at a time when condoms (made of animal skin or cloth) were expensive and contraception was denounced by the Catholic Church. (By the 1800s, all types of contraception were illegal in the United States, Europe, and Canada; in some places, these laws stayed on the books until the 1940s.)

7. He was a fugitive.

In 1755, an Italian inquisition arrested Casanova and tried him for committing numerous acts of adultery (under the guise of charging him with witchcraft). Casanova was sentenced to five years at the Leads, one of Italy's most secure prisons, named for the lead that covered its walls. But Casanova managed what no one before him had done: he broke out of the Leads. He found an iron rod in the prison yard, turned it into a digging tool, and then convinced a monk in a neighboring cell to dig a tunnel that connected their cells and also led to the outside world. Eleven months later, he crawled out of the prison to freedom. Casanova fled to France where he traveled; worked as a translator, librarian, and writer; and lived until his death in 1798.

Viva Las Vegas!

More than 3 million couples have tied the knot in Las Vegas since the city's founding in 1905. With more than 120,000 weddings performed there annually, Sin City is America's unassailable wedding capital.

Here's what you'll need to get married in Vegas: two forms of ID, about $100, a witness, and your future spouse. There's no blood test required for marriages in Nevada, and the Marriage Bureau is open until midnight every day (including holidays) for your convenience. Unless you choose a busy night, the entire process should take less than an hour.

Loving You Tender
The most popular way to get married in Vegas is at an Elvis Presley–themed ceremony (meaning a minister or justice of the peace administers the vows and an Elvis impersonator is the witness and entertainment). But there's one man who acts as both "Elvis" and minister. Norm Jones works at the Graceland Wedding Chapel, the Flamingo Garden Chapel, and the Chapel of Love. He's been a professional Elvis since he was 18 years old and has been the "Presley of the Pulpit" since he was ordained in 1994. Jones, who will happily croon a tune for your big

day, says the most popular songs requests are "Can't Help Falling in Love" and "Love Me Tender."

Variety Is the Spice of Life

But Elvis isn't the only game in town. In fact, there are almost as many ways to get married in Las Vegas as there are Elvis impersonators. Here are a few:

- At a drive-through. Works just the same as for a burger—drive your car right up to the minister's window. No need to unbuckle your seat belt to tie the knot.
- On the deck of a ship at Treasure Island with a pirate officiating. For a little extra, another pirate will swing down from the rigging with the ring.
- Atop a half-scale replica of the Eiffel Tower at the Paris Las Vegas Hotel.
- In one of the world's most garish combinations of gilt, fresco, and glitter: Liberace's mansion.
- At the Flamingo Casino's Flamingo Garden, surrounded by the pink long-legged birds and by penguins.
- At the Las Vegas Hilton, on the bridge of the starship *Enterprise*. You can have Klingons present—or Ferengi, if you prefer—with the reception at *Deep Space Nine*'s Quark's bar.

The Stars Come Out

Regular Joes and Janes aren't the only people who've made marrying in Las Vegas an event. Hollywood celebrities have been doing it for decades. In the 1930s, when Hollywood was turning out its first superstars, Las Vegas, just 275 miles away, was an easy place to get a quickie marriage away from the paparazzi's glare. And when California added a mandatory blood test for all marriage licenses, Vegas became *the* place for Californians (famous or not) to get married.

- Elvis himself married Priscilla in Vegas in 1967, though he borrowed the $15 for the license.
- Bing Crosby, Clint Eastwood, Zsa Zsa Gabor, Jon Bon Jovi, and Michael Jordan have all gotten married in Las Vegas.
- A few stars liked it so much, they kept coming back. After *Psycho*'s Janet Leigh and Tony Curtis split, they both headed to Vegas for their next marriages. Curtis returned to marry again in 1968 . . . and in 1993. Leigh also wed her next husband, stockbroker Robert Brandt, in Las Vegas; that marriage stuck. And Mickey Rooney married his third, fourth, sixth, and seventh wives in Vegas.
- Not all Vegas marriages are short-lived, though—Paul Newman and Joanne Woodward are still married, almost 50 years after their Vegas wedding.

Niagara's for Newlyweds

*After your Las Vegas nuptials, you may want to head off
to Niagara Falls for the honeymoon because, as Virginia Hogan,
who honeymooned there in 1946, reflected, if a newlywed
couple doesn't make the pilgrimage to the falls, "they may
as well have a wedding cake without the icing."*

Who exactly were the first honeymooners to visit
Niagara Falls? No one's sure. Some say that Aaron
Burr's daughter Theodosia and her husband Joseph Alston
came in 1801. Others mention Jerome Bonaparte (brother
to French emperor Napoléon) and his American wife
Elizabeth Patterson, who visited in 1803. No matter, in
the early 1800s, Niagara Falls was a popular stop for
wealthy honeymooners. By the 1900s, couples of all economic classes were flocking to the falls, making it the
world's premier honeymoon resort.

Why Niagara?

At first glance, this natural wonder on the New York–
Canada border doesn't seem like an obvious choice for
romance. In fact, it's better known today as the place where
daredevils climbed into barrels or onto tightropes and tried
to conquer nature, or as the site of a massive hydroelectric
power plant. But in an era before most people could afford to

travel to exotic places like the Caribbean or Hawaii, Niagara Falls was an accessible vacation spot, and anyone with a car could get there.

Certificates and Contests

Local promoters went to great lengths to boost Niagara Falls' image as a honeymoon destination. For years, the train from New York City to Niagara Falls was called the "Honeymoon Special" (it now has a far less evocative name: the "Lake Shore Limited"). In 1939, telephone poles from Syracuse and Rochester to the falls proclaimed the route the "Honeymoon Trail." And in 1941, the Niagara Falls, New York, Chamber of Commerce held a contest to find the oldest living Niagara Falls honeymooners. The winners: octogenarians Mr. and Mrs. Albert Praul of Philadelphia, who honeymooned there in 1876.

But by far, the longest-running and most popular promotional gimmick is the honeymoon certificate. All honeymooners at the falls get a certificate to commemorate the event. The certificate was first offered in Niagara Falls, New York, in 1940 (Niagara Falls, Ontario, quickly adopted it as well). Eleven years later, the Niagara Falls, Ontario, Chamber of Commerce estimated that 4,000 certificates were awarded annually. The local press feted the first couple to receive one—and the 1,000th and the 2,000th and the 10,000th. And newspapers celebrated the first Alaskan couple, the first Israeli couple, and the first couple to arrive on motorcycles.

Hollywood Comes to Niagara

Niagara Falls has also hosted many celebrities and has been memorialized in pop culture:

- In the 1930s, Prince and Princess Takamatsu of Japan and Prince and Princess Asturias of Spain honeymooned there.
- In 1949, Canadian prime minister Louis St. Laurent attended a business meeting in Niagara Falls. He brought his wife along, and local papers announced that the couple was celebrating a honeymoon—even though the St. Laurents had been married for 41 years.
- Niagara Falls appears in the 1928 movie *The Crowd* and the 1953 Marilyn Monroe film *Niagara*. It's also mentioned in Alfred Hitchcock's *To Catch a Thief*. And when Superman finally won of the heart of Lois Lane in *Superman II*, the pair was staying in a honeymoon suite at Niagara Falls.
- Frank Sinatra ("Let's Get Away from It All") and the musical *Guys and Dolls* ("Adelaide's Lament") memorialize the falls in songs.
- Niagara Falls, New York, was the setting of the short-lived 2004 TV series *Wonderfalls*.

"It is wisdom to believe the heart."

—*George Santayana, writer*

It Happened in History

Valentine's Day is more than just candy and roses. Here are some of the historic events that took place on February 14.

1849
James Polk sat for the first presidential photograph.

1859
Oregon became the United States' 33rd state.

1876
Alexander Graham Bell applied to patent the telephone.

1886
The first trainload of California oranges left Los Angeles for the eastern United States via the Transcontinental Railroad.

1895
The Importance of Being Earnest, by Oscar Wilde, opened at the St. James Theatre in London.

1896
Prince Edward of Wales (later king of England) rode in a motor vehicle; he was the first member of the British royal family to do so.

1899

Congress approved the use of voting machines for federal elections.

1912

Arizona became the United States' 48th state.

1919

The United Parcel Service (UPS) was formed.

1929

In Chicago, members of Al Capone's gang killed seven members of a rival gang led by George "Bugs" Moran.

1939

Victor Fleming replaced George Cukor as director of *Gone With the Wind*.

1962

The first televised tour of the White House aired, led by First Lady Jacqueline Kennedy.

1988

Fifty-year-old Bobby Allison won the Daytona 500; he was the oldest driver to do so.

1990

The *Voyager I* space probe photographed our entire solar system.

From Currency to Kisses

You probably didn't give it much thought the last time you bought truffles for your sweetheart, but the history of chocolate is almost as rich and satisfying as the taste of chocolate itself.

600

The Maya established cacao plantations in Central America after harvesting wild cacao beans for hundreds of years. They used cacao to make *chocol haa*, a hot, frothy beverage flavored with vanilla, hot chili powder, and other spices. But only Mayan royalty were allowed to drink chocol haa; everyone else had to settle for *balche*, a fermented beverage made from honey and bark.

1200

The Aztecs also had a cacao drink, *cacahuatl*, a chocolate beverage they believed the god Quetzalcoatl had given their ancestors. But unlike the Maya, the Aztecs preferred cacahuatl cold. The Aztecs also used cacao beans as currency and collected them as tribute from the tribes they dominated.

1500s

The first shipments of cacao beans arrived in Europe from Central and South America in 1585. At this time, chocolate was appreciated mostly for its "medicinal" value. "This drink is the healthiest thing, and the greatest sustenance of anything you could drink in the world," one chocolate advocate wrote, "because he who drinks a cup of this liquid, no matter how far he walks, can go a whole day without eating anything else."

1650–1727

In the late 1600s, chocolate began appearing as a flavoring in food. In France, you could buy chocolate biscuits; in Spain, chocolate rolls and cakes. In Italy, you could order chocolate soup, chocolate liver, and chocolate pasta—including chocolate lasagna. Then, in 1727, an Englishman named Nicholas Sanders became the first person, as far as historians can tell, to make a hot chocolate drink using milk instead of water. But you still couldn't find a chocolate bar because nobody knew how to make chocolate in solid form.

1828–1847

Then, in 1828, a Dutch chemist named Coenraad Johannes Van Houten invented a hydraulic press that could remove fatty cocoa butter from the ground cacao beans. This left behind a solid "cake" that could then be ground into a fine cocoa powder.

Nineteen years later, English chocolate maker Francis Fry figured out a way to combine cocoa powder and sugar with melted cocoa butter to create a chocolate paste that could be pressed into molds and formed into solid shapes. This was the world's first eating chocolate.

1879

After several years of collaborating with chemist Henri Nestlé, Swiss chocolate maker Daniel Peter finally figured out how to add powdered milk (which Nestlé had invented the year before) to chocolate. This was the world's first milk chocolate.

That same year, another Swiss chocolate maker, Rudolphe Lindt, invented a process he called "conching." Until then, chocolate was coarse and gritty, kind of like granulated sugar. Lindt's conching process crushed chocolate paste beneath huge granite rollers for more than 72 hours, at which point the particles became so tiny and smooth that the resulting chocolate melted in your mouth.

1893

Next came Milton Snavely Hershey, owner of the world's largest caramel factory, who visited the 1893 World's Columbian Exposition in Chicago and saw a demonstration of chocolate-making machinery. Hershey was so impressed that when the exhibition closed, he bought the machinery and began making chocolate-coated caramels. In 1900, he sold his caramel company and focused exclusively on chocolate. Hershey manufactured chocolate on such an enormous scale—as much as 100,000 pounds of it everyday—that he could offer it more cheaply to the consumer. He priced his Hershey bars at just a nickel each; they sold at that price until 1969.

1917 and on

During the early 20th century, most people considered chocolate to be a treat more for kids than adults. That changed during World War I, when the government sent chocolate to soldiers in battle. Why? It was cheap, it didn't spoil, and its high sugar content provided a quick energy boost.

During World War II, American soldiers brought chocolate with them wherever they went. In Europe, G.I.s mostly carried Hershey bars, but soldiers in tropical regions like North Africa and the South Pacific ate M&M's, because they didn't melt as easily as chocolate bars. During the war, the U.S. Air Force was the largest purchaser of M&M's; the Army was the number two customer.

The average G.I. consumed 50 pounds of candy and chocolate a year, three times what he had eaten before the war. And he brought his appetite for chocolate home with him. It wasn't just for kids anymore.

Romancing the Cinema

*Romantic movies have been around since filmmaking began,
and some of the most famous have marked the eras in which they
were produced. Here's a time line of our favorite romantic films.*

1896: *The Kiss*

Probably the earliest "love story" caught on film, this 20-second film was a reenactment of the final scene of the 1895 Broadway play *The Widow Jones*. It was also the most popular film made by Thomas Edison's film company (called the Edison Manufacturing Company) and was filmed at Edison's famous Black Maria studio in West Orange, New Jersey. *The Kiss* was just that: a close-up of a kiss between Mary Irwin and John C. Rice, stars of the Broadway show. The short film produced many firsts: it included the first on-screen kiss, it was the first film to be criticized for being too racy, and it was the first movie to spawn a censorship discussion among lawmakers and the public.

1921: *The Sheik*

Absolutes are sketchy in the world of early filmmaking, but *The Sheik*, starring Rudolf Valentino, was probably the first romance/adventure film. The movie tells the story of Sheik Ahmed (Valentino), who falls in love with a British socialite named Diana (played by Agnes Ayres), kidnaps her, and takes her to his palace. At first, Diana rebuffs the Sheik's advances, but she soon discovers that she loves him as fiercely as he does her. This movie launched not only the epic romance genre but the career of the Italian-born Valentino, nicknamed the "Latin Lover" and considered by many to be one of history's most popular male heartthrobs—if not the first.

1936: *Camille*

"Don't leave me, Marguerite!" So cried Robert Taylor at the end of this tearjerker that epitomized the age of melodramatic movies in the 1930s. In fact, many movie critics consider *Camille* to be one of modern filmmaking's most tragic romantic love stories. George Cukor's film tells the story of a 19th-century French courtesan, Marguerite Gautier (played by Greta Garbo), who falls in love with a young nobleman (Taylor). Given the societal constraints of the time, the pair is doomed never to be together, and even though they try to overcome the obstacles and look as though they might succeed, Marguerite's dramatic consumptive death at the end renders their love hopeless. The film was based on a novel by Alexandre Dumas *fils*, *La Dame aux Camélias (The Woman with Camelias)*, and the title character was loosely based on a woman Dumas actually knew in Paris, a courtesan named Marie Alphonsine du Plessis, who died of tuberculosis at the age of 24.

1942: *Casablanca*

Often called one of the greatest films of all time, this story of Rick (Humphrey Bogart), Ilsa (Ingrid Bergman), and a supporting cast of unforgettable characters dealing with war, politics, espionage, and lost love is most certainly one of America's most beloved and oft-quoted romantic movies. *Casablanca* was a big-budget picture for its time, especially given that it was a romantic movie instead of an epic. It cost about $1 million to make but was an immediate hit and took in nearly $4 million in box office sales. It also won three Academy Awards (including Best Picture) and produced a hit song, "As Time Goes By," which stayed atop the music charts for 21 weeks in 1942 and 1943.

1961: *Splendor in the Grass*

Director Elia Kazan's film, based on William Inge's Pulitzer Prize–winning play of the same name, was controversial and daring for its time. The movie's theme of sexual repression was rarely discussed in mainstream America and even more rarely appeared on film. The story centers on small-town teens Bud (Warren Beatty) and Deanie (Natalie Wood) growing up in 1920s Kansas. Despite their prudish and classist parents and a society that promotes sex but also condemns it, their love affair is passionate and steamy: *Splendor in the Grass* was the first American film to show a French kiss on-screen and, in its uncut version, one of the first to feature nudity.

The scene of a frantic and naked Natalie Wood running from the bathroom (where she had been in the tub and was fighting with her mother) to her bedroom (where she throws herself on her bed, overcome with teenage angst) showed Wood's bare legs and backside. But that proved too racy for Hollywood censors, so Kazan had to cut the scene before it hit the theaters.

1970: *Love Story*

Oh, the romance . . . oh, the tragedy! The American Film Institute calls *Love Story* one of the most romantic films of all time; it's certainly one of the saddest. The story begins as a typical "boy meets girl": Oliver (Ryan O'Neal) meets Jennifer (Ali MacGraw) in college. The two fall in love, marry, and hope to start a family. But then tragedy strikes. Jennifer has leukemia, can't have children, and soon dies. Despite the downer plot and criticisms of clichéd writing, *Love Story* became the first romance film blockbuster. It was the top-grossing film of 1970 and actually rescued Paramount Studios (which produced the film) from bankruptcy.

1997: *Titanic*

The night that unsinkable ship went down has been chronicled in several movies since 1912, but the 1997 version put a love story at the center of the tragedy and ensured James Cameron's three-hour epic a place in film history books. *Titanic*'s accomplishments read like a seemingly endless string of superlatives: most expensive film of its time ($200 million to make), highest grossing (more than $1 billion worldwide), record number of Academy Award nominations (14; a tie with 1950's *All About Eve*), record wins (11; a tie with 1959's *Ben Hur* and 2004's *Lord of the Rings: Return of the King*), longest cinematic release (it stayed in theaters for 281 days), and longest time atop the U.S. box office (*Titanic* was number one for 15 consecutive weeks).

An English professor wrote the words "Woman without her man is nothing" on the blackboard and asked his students to punctuate it correctly.

The men wrote: "Woman, without her man, is nothing."

The women wrote: "Woman: Without her, man is nothing."

Public Proposals

*Asking a woman to marry you used to be a solemn, private
matter. No longer. Now it's a public event. (Incidentally,
the answers to these proposals were all "yes"!)*

Dan Caplis
Proposed: On television
Story: Caplis and Aimee Sporer worked for Channel 4
News in Denver—he was the legal expert, she was the
anchorwoman. One night, they were sitting next to each
other during a broadcast. After finishing his segment,
Caplis looked at the camera and told the audience that
since they were like family, he wanted to share an important moment with them. He took a ring out of his pocket
and put it in front of Sporer. Choked up, she said, "I
would love to marry you," and then turned away from the
camera. The quick-thinking cameraman cut for a commercial break.

Lou Droesch
Proposed: At a city council meeting
Story: Pam Ferris, the city clerk of Louisville, Colorado,
was taking notes at the council meeting when Droesch,
a local mortgage banker, went up to the microphone to
voice his opinion about an issue. It wasn't the issue

anyone expected. He said, "I'm crazy about your city clerk. And I ask that the city fathers approve my asking for her hand in marriage." Then he got down on one knee and popped the question.

Neil Nathanson

Proposed: In a crossword puzzle
Story: Neil and his girlfriend, Leslie Hamilton, liked doing the *San Francisco Examiner* crossword puzzles together. Michael Kernan wrote in *Smithsonian* magazine that

> one Sunday, Leslie noticed that many of the puzzle answers struck close to home. "State or quarterback" turned out to be MONTANA, which is where she came from. "Instrument" was CELLO, which she plays. "I was about halfway through the puzzle," she remembers, "when I figured out that a string of letters running across the middle of the puzzle said 'DEAR— WILL YOU MARRY ME NEIL.'"

Neil, it turns out, had been working with Merl Reagle, the *Examiner*'s puzzle maker, for four months. They invited him to the wedding. "I never did finish the puzzle," Leslie added.

Jim Bederka

Proposed: During a college graduation ceremony
Story: Paige Griffin was sitting with her class, ready to graduate from Ramapo College in Mahwah, New Jersey,

when her boyfriend Jim showed up and asked her to leave the group for a minute. She said no—she didn't want to cause a disturbance. He kept insisting, getting more and more aggravated. Finally, she gave in. As she stepped into the aisle, she saw two trumpeters decked in medieval garb standing at the stage. Between them, a sign read: "Paige, will you marry me?" When she accepted, the trumpeters held up a "She said yes" sign, and the crowd that had gathered (about 1,500 people) applauded.

Bob Bornack

Proposed: On a billboard

Story: In the Chicago suburb of Wood Dale, Bornack put up a billboard that read: "Teri, Please Marry Me! Love, Bob." The sign company immediately got 10 calls from women named Teri who wanted to know if it was "their" Bob. "One Teri called in a total panic because she's dating two Bobs," said an employee. "She didn't know which one to answer." (It wasn't either of them.)

To read about more proposals, turn to page 158.

In 1228, Scottish women won the legal right to propose marriage. From Scotland, the practice spread throughout the Western world.

Down with Love

Love songs can't always be pretty. See if you can match these anti-love tunes with their descriptions.

A. "Love Stinks" (J. Geils Band)
B. "These Boots Are Made for Walking" (Nancy Sinatra)
C. "Every Breath You Take" (The Police)
D. "Ex-Girlfriend" (No Doubt)
E. "Love Hurts" (Gram Parsons)
F. "Ever Fallen in Love" (Pete Yorn)

1. This empowering tune was first recorded in 1966 and was later covered by Jessica Simpson for the *Dukes of Hazzard* movie soundtrack.

2. This song has been featured in *Can't Hardly Wait* and other angst-ridden films, and the man who wrote and recorded it is often called one of the creators of country-rock, a musical genre in which musicians play country music but use instruments and exhibit the energy usually associated with rock 'n' roll stars.

3. In the film *Shrek 2*, this song appears during a scene in which the film's main characters (Shrek and his new bride

Fiona) contemplate the difficulties that their differences (he's a common ogre; she's a princess) bring to their relationship.

4. This fast-paced, drum-heavy song vents frustration after the end of a long relationship. Many people believed that the person for whom this song was written was the lead singer's bandmate (and former boyfriend), but in fact, the diatribe was aimed at someone else.

5. At first glance, this ballad seems like the love song of a devoted partner. But on closer examination, it's about the end of an obsessive love affair. The band's lead singer penned it during the breakup of his first marriage.

6. A favorite anti-love song as well as an oft-used phrase, this tune appeared both in a movie that bears its title and *The Wedding Singer,* in which Adam Sandler shrilly covers it during a wedding reception scene.

For answers, turn to page 174.

The world's most expensive wedding took place in June 2004 at the Vaux-le-Vicomte palace in France. Indian-born British billionaire Lakshmi Mittal threw the $60 million wedding for his daughter Vanisha. The engagement reception was the day before . . . at Versailles.

Love Potions

Oysters are a well-known aphrodisiac, but here
are two others that might surprise you.

Cockle Bread

In the 17th century, unmarried women in England took
literally the adage that the way to a man's heart is through
his stomach, and they baked bread with "erotic imprints."
After preparing the dough, the women pressed it to themselves, forming an unmistakable shape. Then, they baked
the loaf, called *cockle bread*, and gave it as a gift to the
young men whose attentions they coveted.

Garlic

In ancient Greece and Egypt, people ate garlic daily, in
part because they believed in the plant's powers as an
aphrodisiac. Greek doctors even prescribed the odiferous
bulb as a "stimulant" for men who wanted to increase
their stamina. Many modern herbalists agree with their
ancient counterparts and insist that ingesting large quan-
tities of garlic can combat impotency because garlic
increases blood flow. Careful, though—too much garlic is
also likely to scare off many potential mates.

Love those "I ♥" Bumper Stickers?

Thank New York, New York!

The 1970s were not kind to New York City. Crime was at an all-time high, and the city's finances were at an all-time low. Tourism in the once-glamorous "Big Apple" was slumping badly. So in 1976 the State of New York took action, hiring the Madison Avenue ad agency of Wells, Rich, and Greene to come up with a campaign to restore the city's positive image. The ad execs proposed a simple, four-word slogan—"I Love New York"—and asked graphic artist Milton Glaser, renowned art director for *New York* magazine covers for *Time* and *The Nation*, to come up with the design. He simplified the phrase even more, and "I ♥ NY" was born.

Keep It Simple

This image—properly termed a "rebus" (the representation of words in the form of symbols or pictures)—was an immediate success. It was soon emblazoned on shirts, buttons, calendars, coffee mugs, and bumper stickers all over the city. Ex-Beatle John Lennon, who spent the last years of his life in New York, often wore the famous white T-shirt with the red heart and black lettering.

Glaser's simple design has become the most recognizable, and most imitated, logo in history. A lifelong New Yorker, Glaser received no profit from the sale of items sporting his design.

New York State fared better. The "I Love New York" campaign was an enormous success and a financial boon for the entire state. The New York State Department of Economic Development owns the official rights to the trademark and is supposed to profit every time an "I ♥ " item is sold. To date, the agency has received more than $1 million from licenses to use the design (and has filed more than 3,000 grievances against imitators who have tried to use the logo without paying for it).

I ♥ New York More Than Ever

After the September 11, 2001, terrorist attacks destroyed the World Trade Center, Glaser and his "I ♥ " campaign again came to the city's aid. He revamped the logo to include a small black smudge (a "wound") in the lower left-hand part of the heart—geographically, the place in the city where the twin towers once stood.

Glaser sent his revised logo, again pro bono, to the *New York Daily News*, which printed nearly 1 million small posters that were wrapped around one issue of the newspaper. The new logo was soon seen throughout the city, tacked on walls and hanging in windows. Today, many people continue to display this new logo—and the old one—as a show of support for New York City residents.

A Trying Affair

*Love letters should be private, but they don't always
stay that way. And dastardly things can happen when
romantic communiqués become the talk of the town.*

In 1567, a small gilded box arrived in England. The 20
missives within were evidence for the murder trial of
Mary, Queen of Scots. But the letters—filled with passionate language and poetry and detailing an affair between
the queen and the Earl of Bothwell—were controversial:
their veracity was questioned even then, but Britons
rushed to judgment and the queen ultimately lost her
throne . . . and her head.

The Crime
In February 1566, assassins sprinkled gunpowder in an
Edinburgh, Scotland, house where Lord Darnley, second
husband to Mary, Queen of Scots, was sleeping. The assassins lit the powder, and moments later, an explosion lev-
eled the home. Darnley was found dead outside.

The Accused
The Earl of Bothwell and Queen Mary herself. Mary's
Scottish subjects suspected that the couple was involved
in an affair, and Mary's reaction to her husband's death

(she never condemned the murder and married Bothwell soon after) seemed suspicious.

The Evidence

Bothwell was tried first, and the evidence against him was circumstantial. He was one of only a few nobles loyal to the queen, and Darnley hadn't been a particularly good husband. In fact, a year before, Darnley had conspired with a group trying to overthrow Mary; they'd killed her personal secretary and then imprisoned the queen in her palace. Mary ultimately escaped, but Bothwell, loyal to his royal lover, had both the motive and opportunity to kill Darnley. The case was weak, though, and in the end, Bothwell was acquitted of the crime.

Mary was tried next—in England, where she'd escaped to hide out with her cousin Queen Elizabeth in the hope of avoiding prosecution. The cousins didn't really get along (Elizabeth was a Protestant and Mary was a Catholic at a time when the two religious groups were vying for control in Great Britain), but Mary had hoped Elizabeth would offer refuge. It seemed at first that she might be safe, but then those damning love letters surfaced, and Mary went on trial.

The letters—called the "casket letters" because they were stored in a silver casket, or chest—were allegedly written by Mary to Bothwell. They "proved" that the pair was indeed having an affair, and they were all that was necessary for the Protestant English to demand a trial for the Catholic Scottish queen.

The Verdict

In 1567, Queen Elizabeth imprisoned her cousin and convened a tribunal to try Mary for murder. Mary wasn't allowed to testify or see the casket letters, the only evidence against her. Ultimately, the letters didn't show a clear link between the lovers and the murder, and many suspected they were forgeries. Even Elizabeth herself questioned the letters' authenticity: their origins were shady (nobles loyal to Darnley claimed to have "found" them), and they were riddled with poor grammar, mistakes the well-educated Mary would never have made. Eventually, the court was unable to prove that Mary had conspired with Bothwell to murder Darnley.

The Aftermath

Mary was off the hook for Darnley's murder, but she wasn't free. Once Elizabeth had her Catholic cousin in her clutches, she decided to keep Mary imprisoned under house arrest; this way, Elizabeth could assure Protestant rule in England and solidify her own power base. For the next 18 years, Mary tried to escape. She also conspired to overthrow her cousin and take the English throne. Finally, in 1587, one of her plots was intercepted. Mary, Queen of Scots, was convicted of treason and beheaded.

The love letters that had been the catalyst for her fate disappeared, and today, only copies exist. Most modern historians agree with Queen Elizabeth and the 16th century tribunal that Mary didn't write the letters, and more than 400 years later, no one knows for sure who did.

The Finer Points of "Fan Flirting"

During the Victorian era (1837–1901), courting became strict and formalized; debutante balls, calling cards, and chaperones were the norm. But men and women developed ways around the rules. One involved women using fans as a flirting tool. Below are some of the ways women used their fans to communicate with the opposite sex. Take note, fellas.

Fan Action	Meaning
Slow fanning	I am engaged.
In front of the face with right hand	Please approach me.
In front of the face with left hand	Leave me alone.
Open, then shut	I want to be kissed.
Open wide	I love you.
Half open	Let's just be friends.
Closed	I don't like you at all.

More Prime Time Dating

*Reality dating show contestants continue their quests
for love on the tube. (Part 1 is on page 14.)*

Who Wants to Marry My Dad?

Premiered: July 14, 2003
Average number of viewers: 9.3 million

Adult children match up their single fathers in the
aptly named *Who Wants to Marry My Dad?* The female
suitors face lie detector tests and outrageous challenges—
like integrating the word "bald" as many times as possible
over lunch with a bald bachelor. On this program, the
stars are older folks with families, a demographic that had
previously been absent from reality dating shows.

This show lasted only two seasons, and contrary to its
title, marriage didn't result from either. The first ended with
wealthy businessman Don Mueller proposing to Christena
Ferran, who declined and chose to remain in her hometown
of San Diego (Mueller lived in Cincinnati). The next year,
three daughters scoured the land—or the 13-woman contestant pool—for a woman to marry their dad, Marty Okland.
The daughters chose Stacy Leutner. Okland did propose, but
the pair ultimately split up. Apparently, even lie detectors
and trickery can't guarantee a successful union.

Average Joe

Premiered: November 3, 2003
Average number of viewers: 10 million

In this twist on *The Bachelor, Average Joe* originally offered up an attractive female contestant who had to choose from a gaggle of so-called geek suitors (the format changed slightly in season three when the geek was the contestant, and the beauties the suitors, but returned to the original format the next year). Once the beauty began to bond with the geeks, a group of suave, attractive male models arrived. The show's inherent question—"Would an attractive person choose an average-looking person with an exquisite personality over an attractive person who is lacking a great personality?"—played out for all of America to see.

In the first two seasons, the geeks lost to a stud, disappointing underdogs everywhere. Just as the series seemed to prove that nice guys finish last, Adam Mesh, an average Joe who had been snubbed earlier, became the third season's bachelor. Despite the show's efforts to sabotage his dates, Mesh won the heart of beautiful suitor Samantha Trenk. Then, finally, in the fourth season, model Anna Chudoba chose an average Joe over a stud. When the shows ended, though, none of these relationships took off.

Drinking the Stars

No romantic celebration would be complete without the aristocrat of wines . . . the bubbly beverage of love . . . champagne.

Those Pesky Bubbles

Champagne, France, is the country's northernmost grape-growing area. For centuries, Benedictine monks at the region's Abbey Hautvillers produced fine wines for the church's holy sacraments and Europe's nobility. The monks produced still wines (without bubbles) . . . rather, they tried to. The abbey was having a problem with batches of unintentionally carbonated wine.

Usually, before wine is bottled, the grape juice has fermented, meaning that yeast on the grape skins has turned the fruits' sugars into alcohol. But grapes ripen slowly in Champagne's northern vineyards, and the monks had to harvest them late in the growing season. Winter cold sometimes halted the fermentation process—after the grapes had been crushed but before the wine went into bottles. Then when spring warmed up the wine, it finished fermenting, trapping carbon dioxide gas inside the glass bottles. This gas produced fizzing bubbles and built up pressure that could push out corks or even cause the bottles to explode (phenomena the monks called "mad wine").

Star Struck

In 1688, a monk named Pierre Pérignon became treasurer of the abbey, and his job included overseeing the wine operations. At first, he experimented with ways to prevent carbonation from fizzing up in the abbey's wine, but sometime during his 47 years at the monastery, he gained an affinity for the sparkling wine. According to legend, he was so enamored with the drink that, the first time he tried it, he called out to his fellow monks, "Come quickly, I am drinking the stars!"

Soon, Dom Pérignon tamed the mad wine into delicious champagne. He used rope and wire to keep the bottles corked and thicker glass bottles to prevent explosions. He also perfected champagne by blending multiple grapes from different vineyards to create the drink's signature taste and developed a method of producing a clear, straw-colored champagne from black grapes. Champagne soon became a favorite drink of English and French royalty.

Blue-Chip Bubbly

Today, Pérignon's name and techniques are still attached to fine champagne, even though he died in 1715 and was buried at his beloved Abbey Hautvillers. In 1794, wine trader Claude Moët bought the abbey and its vineyards. His family's company (which became Moët et Chandon in 1832) continued to create the prestigious champagne. In 1921, to honor both the company's history and the monk many people call "the Father of Champagne," they named their finest vintage Dom Pérignon.

Considered by many wine critics (and brides and grooms) to be the best champagne in the world, Dom Pérignon has become a symbol of love and luxury. A gift bottle of 1998 Dom Pérignon (the champagne's finest year) can set you back about $140, and a special 1998 edition Dom Pérignon (presented in a gold-studded bottle designed by Karl Lagerfeld) goes for a whopping $1,915.

Bad Dates: One Wine-y Fella

"It was a blind date. He brought red wine to a friend's housewarming party and proceeded to get very drunk, very fast. When he tripped over the host's sleeping cocker spaniel during a round of karaoke, upending his wine glass (and the bottle he was carrying) all over himself and the white walls, I knew we were done before we began."

—*Sophie A.*

Weird Weddings

Getting hitched no longer requires a traditional ceremony.
Here are some couples who found unique ways to
declare their love for each other.

Till Freefall Do Us Part

If you've ever wondered what it would feel like to get married while plummeting toward the earth, you're not alone. Every year, hundreds of couples decide to get hitched while flying through the air. Most have a brief ceremony in the airplane on the way up to the jump altitude and then take the plunge. But others, like Utah residents and expert skydivers Lance and Heather Baites, get married during the drop. Their maneuver had to be carefully rehearsed to ensure everyone's safety, and a justice of the peace, a maid of honor, and a best man all dove with the couple to act as witnesses.

Underwater "I Do's"

On New Year's Eve 1999, Canadians Ghislain Rivard and Ghislaine La Rouche decided to renew their wedding vows 26 feet under the Indian Ocean off the coast of Indonesia. They had married 10 years before aboard a cruise ship and decided they wanted the ocean to play an even bigger role in their vow renewal. So the happy couple dressed in full traditional wedding gear, used weights to keep them underwater, and breathed using tubes attached to overhead air tanks. An underwater gazebo and an altar for the minister to preside over the participants were set up by staff at the Indonesian dive center where the couple trained for the special ceremony. And the groom and bride used waterproof boards to write out their vows.

Naked Nuptials

Every year on Valentine's Day, couples vacationing at the Hedonism III resort in St. Ann, Jamaica, can get married in nothing but their birthday suits. In February 2001, eleven such events took place there in what *Playboy* magazine called "the world's largest nude wedding." The resort provides all the services for the weddings, including marriage licenses, a minister, a cake, and witnesses. Dresses and tuxedoes are optional.

Up, Up, and "I Do"!

On January 9, 2003, Chutrudee Sukhajati and Peter Kotize exchanged vows and rings on a flight in a hot-air balloon above the city of Chiang Mai, Thailand. Kotize had proposed two years before during another balloon ride—that time, above Nepal and in sight of Mount Everest—and the couple wanted to marry the same way. Their one-hour wedding flight took off before sunrise; the bride, groom, chief registrar, captain, and three cameramen all crowded into the basket. While in flight, the couple signed their official marriage registration document. The balloon then landed in a nearby field, where the captain presented the newlyweds with a wedding cake and champagne breakfast as a start to their honeymoon.

He Proposes, He Scores!

On January 17, 2004, hockey fans Dan and Darla Stratton of Ontario, Canada, married at center ice in a local hockey arena. They employed the services of Wayne Prevett, a wedding officiant and fellow hockey fan who runs his own company that caters to unique theme weddings. The bride wore both a traditional wedding dress and a Toronto Maple Leafs sweater. The groom wore a solid-gold tuxedo in honor of flamboyant Canadian hockey commentator Don Cherry, known for his extravagant on-air wardrobe. Prevett presided over the ceremony dressed in a referee's uniform. Five groomsmen and five bridesmaids donned skates and stood at center ice to observe the ceremony. Area residents also packed the arena to watch the wedding and even started a round of the wave to help the Strattons celebrate.

The phrase "tying the knot" comes from an ancient Irish tradition called "handfasting," in which a Druid priest tied the hands of the bride and groom together during the wedding ceremony.

Dating By the Numbers

It's gotten a lot more complicated than "Pick you up at eight."

1 hour
Average time it takes a woman to decide if she wants to see a man again. Men take an average of 15 minutes to decide if they want to see a woman again.

8 minutes
Time potential couples spend together during a round of speed dating

12.5 percent
Chance that a first date will call for a second date after 24 hours have passed

17 percent
Chance that someone will like a date set up by a friend

30 hours
The longest kiss on record. The smooch, between 19-year-old Louisa Almedovar and her 22-year-old boyfriend Rich Langley, took place in 2001 at a TV studio in New York as

part of a Valentine's Day special. The couple didn't sit down, eat, or visit the bathroom for the entire time.

34
Number of facial muscles used during passionate kissing

35 percent
Middle-aged American women who say they'd prefer to date younger men

72 percent
Italian men who, when asked to rate their kisses on a scale of 10, awarded themselves either a 9 or 10

10,113
Number of virgins worldwide who bought an insurance policy against the possibility of immaculate conception in 2000 (the British insurance company that sold the policies also offers protection against alien abduction and becoming a werewolf).

7 million+
Number of registered users of online dating services

The word "marry" comes from the Latin *maritare*, which means "to become a husband."

The Bigger the Better, Part 2

Our list of famous diamonds continues. (Part 1 is on page 9.)

Most Expensive Royal Tag Sale

A cushion-cut (or rounded rectangle) white diamond of 135.92 carats and impeccable clarity, the "Queen of Holland" takes its name from the Dutch sovereign Queen Wilhelmina, who owned it during her reign from 1890 to 1948. When Wilhelmina stepped down, she sold the diamond to India's Maharajah of Nawanagar, who had it set in a ceremonial necklace. Jeweler Cartier then bought the stone from the Maharajah and sold it in 1978 for a reported $7 million.

Most Famous Diamond

The blue "Hope Diamond" was mined in Golconda, India, and then placed into a statue of the Hindu goddess Sita. But during the 17th century, a Frenchman named Jean Baptiste Tavernier stole it and sold it to France's King Louis XIV. Louis called the stone (all 67 carats of it) the "Blue Diamond of the Crown," and it remained in the French royal family until the French Revolution, when it was stolen again. This time, the diamond's whereabouts remained unknown until 1939, when it turned up in the possession of Henry Philip Hope, a wealthy English banker and the person for whom the stone is now named. The Hope family eventually sold the diamond to Harry Winston, who used it for nearly a decade as a promotional draw for his jewelry company. Then, in 1958, Winston donated the stone to the National Museum of Natural History in Washington, DC. Some people believe Winston donated the stone because he feared that the diamond was cursed (since it had originally been stolen from a religious artifact), but Winston said the donation was an effort to create a national jewel collection for the United States. On November 10, 1958, Winston's company packed the Hope Diamond in a plain brown box and sent it to Washington by registered mail. It arrived safely and remains on display at the Smithsonian today.

Rarest Colored Large Stone

At 182 carats, the "Darya-ye Noor" (Persian for "sea of light") is one of the largest diamonds in the world. It's also the rarest color: pale pink. Darya-ye Noor comes from the Golconda mines in India and changed hands several times over the last three hundred years. It eventually came into the possession of the Shah of Persia (now Iran), Fath Ali Shah Qajar, who ruled from 1797 to 1834. Qajar had his name engraved on one of the facets and wore the stone set in a brooch. Today, the diamond remains in the collection of the Iranian crown jewels.

Helen of Troy

*Her romance with a Trojan prince is often credited
with bringing about one of the greatest defeats in Greek
mythology, but it seems that lust and deception, more
than a passionate love affair, led to the fall of Troy.*

A Bad Apple Strikes Again

Helen's affiliation with the Trojan War was inadvertent.
According to legend, it all started prosaically enough with
a wedding and a spurned guest. When Peleus (a mortal)
married Thetis (a sea goddess), their nuptials were the
social event of the season. The happy couple intended to
invite all of the gods but forgot to send an invitation to
Eris, the goddess of discord. Eris was angry at the slight.
She crashed the wedding, tossed a golden apple onto the
banquet table, and announced that the fruit belonged to
the goddess who was the most beautiful.

Three goddesses reached for the apple: Hera, queen of the
gods; Athena, goddess of wisdom; and Aphrodite, goddess of
love. Naturally, the three began fighting. They appealed to
Zeus to break the deadlock, but he decided to stay out of the
fray. Instead, Zeus suggested that the women ask Paris,
prince of Troy, to arbitrate the celestial beauty contest.

Each goddess offered Paris a bribe: Hera promised him
power, Athena promised wealth and wisdom, and

Aphrodite promised him the mortal world's most beautiful woman: Helen. That last offer proved irresistible, and Paris declared Aphrodite the winner of the golden apple.

But there was a problem—Helen was already married.

Meanwhile, Back in Sparta . . .

Helen was deemed such a catch that, when she reached marriageable age, powerful suitors came from far and wide to claim her. Tyndareus, her father and the king of Sparta, worried about offending those who weren't chosen. Odysseus offered a solution: make every suitor swear an oath to support and protect the man chosen as Helen's husband. Each prospective bridegroom, no doubt thinking he would be the victor, agreed.

Tyndareus chose Menelaus, prince of Mycenae (a city in southern Greece), to be his son-in-law. The union would

unite the two royal families. Although he was considerably older than his bride and reportedly rather dull, Helen dutifully married Menelaus, and when her father died, Menelaus became king of Sparta.

Paris Finally Arrives

Soon thereafter, encouraged by Aphrodite, Paris traveled to Sparta to claim Helen. The prince of Troy didn't communicate his true intentions and instead convinced Menelaus and his court to accept him as a mere visitor. Menelaus entertained Paris for a week before the king was called away on business.

As soon as Menelaus left, Paris made his move and spirited Helen away to Troy, taking much of Menelaus's money with them for good measure. Helen's role in the escape is unclear. Paris was younger and cut a much more dashing figure than Menelaus did, thus many versions of the story hold that Paris and Helen had fallen in love. But others paint Helen as a victim whisked away against her will. And in Euripides' play, *Helen*, the "woman" who accompanied Paris to Troy wasn't even Helen herself but a likeness, fashioned out of clouds by one of the gods. Regardless, when the pair reached Troy, Paris's father married them.

Coalition of the Unwilling

When Menelaus returned and found his wife gone and his treasury looted, he was angry. He remembered the oath Tyndareus had extracted from his rivals. As Menelaus gathered his own forces to attack Troy and bring Helen back, he called on the rivals and held them to their word.

Some of those old suitors tried to renege on the commitment. Odysseus faked insanity. The king of Cyprus initially promised to contribute 50 ships to the effort but, in the end, sent just one . . . and 49 toy boats made out of clay.

War Comes to Troy

Menelaus and his allies launched their assault on Troy in 1194 BC. The war lasted 10 years, and there were many casualties on both sides, including Paris. At the battle's end, Menelaus prepared to make Helen a casualty as well; she had betrayed him, after all. But as Menelaus raised his sword to kill her, he fell under the spell of her beauty and spared her life. Eventually, the two set off for home.

But legend holds that Menelaus neglected to make a sacrifice to the gods for his victory. As retribution, the sea god Poseidon sent a storm to waylay the travelers. In that storm, Menelaus lost 75 ships, and as a result, he and Helen were stranded in Egypt for seven years. Eventually, they returned to Sparta and lived, according to some, happily ever after.

The description of Helen having a "face that launched a thousand ships" is usually attributed to Christopher Marlowe and appears in his 16th-century play, *The Tragical History of Doctor Faustus*.

True Romance, Hollywood Style

*Old Hollywood provides us with some sweeping
love stories. See if you can match these Hollywood
couples to the story of their romance.*

A. Natalie Wood and Robert Wagner
B. Joanne Woodward and Paul Newman
C. Katharine Hepburn and Spencer Tracy
D. Lauren Bacall and Humphrey Bogart
E. Elizabeth Taylor and Richard Burton
F. Lucille Ball and Desi Arnaz
G. Carole Lombard and Clark Gable

1. She's an actress and model best known for her husky
voice and come-hither looks. He was an actor whom the
American Film Institute once called "the greatest male
star of all time." They met on the set of her first film, and
even though he was 25 years her senior, the pair wed in
1945 and remained married until his death from cancer in
1957. For several of those years, they lived in an exclusive
area of Los Angeles called Holmby Hills, where one of
their neighbors was Judy Garland.

2. He's one of Hollywood's most famous and celebrated actors; she's a four-time Academy Award nominee and one-time winner. They met while doing a Broadway play in 1955 and married three years later (the same year she won her Oscar). Despite rumors, tragedies (his son from his first marriage died in 1978), and decades of making movies, they've remained hitched. When asked why he never strayed, this actor's response was, "Why fool around with hamburgers when you have steak at home?" Today, they're as well known for their political activism and philanthropic endeavors as for their years as Hollywood stars.

3. She was a star of stage, screen, and television and was the first woman to head a production company. He was a musician and actor who immigrated to the United States as a teenager. They were married from 1940 to 1960 and had two children. They were also pioneers who starred in one of TV's most popular series and invented many of the techniques now used universally in television production, including using three cameras to film a show, filming before a live audience, using a comic to entertain the audience before filming, and rerunning old episodes.

4. She made her film debut at the age of 12 when a director saw her playing baseball in the street and cast her as a tomboy in his latest picture. He was an Academy Award–winning actor and one of the first true movie stars. They married in 1939 (the year his most famous film was released) and lived on a California ranch until she died in a plane crash three years later. She was buried at the Forest Lawn Memorial Park in Glendale, California, and even though he remarried in 1949 and 1955, when he died in 1960, he too was interred at Forest Lawn . . . right next to her.

5. She was a child star whose "miraculous" early years in Hollywood included making movies with seasoned actors like Edmund Gwenn, Orson Welles, and Rex Harrison. He was a handsome young studio actor who served as a caddie for Clark Gable before finding fame in the movies (one of his most well-known films involved an unsinkable ship). Together, they were a Hollywood glamour couple. They married each other twice (in 1957 and 1972) and raised three daughters. She died in a boating accident in 1981, and even though he remarried nine years later, he still says it's difficult to discuss her death.

6. She was a witty, independent screen legend nominated for 12 Best Actress Academy Awards (she won four times). He was nominated for nine Best Actor awards and won twice. This pair made nine movies together, including one about an interracial romance (quite a scandal for the 1960s). They never married—he already had a wife whom he refused to leave due to his strict Roman Catholic beliefs—but they carried on an affair for more than 20 years.

7. She signed with MGM in 1943 when she was just 11 years old and became one of the best-known child—and then adult—actresses in Hollywood. He was a British stage star whose first notable Hollywood film was a 1952 picture that also starred Olivia de Havilland. Together, this pair was one of Tinseltown's most famous and infamous couples. They wed twice (in 1964 and 1975) and were married for a total of 12 years. They also costarred in one of Hollywood's most expensive films (an epic that cost $44 million to make in 1963) and made more than 10 other movies together throughout their careers.

For answers, turn to page 175.

∞

Quote Me

"It is only with the heart that one can see rightly; what is essential is invisible to the eye."

—*Antoine de Saint Exupery*

"Nobody has ever measured, not even poets, how much the heart can hold."

—*Zelda Fitzgerald*

Honeymoon Trivia

We all know that newlyweds like to celebrate their love by going on a honeymoon. But here are four things you might not know about that postwedding vacation.

- The word "honeymoon" dates back to the 16th century and originally referred to a period of about one month—the cycle of a moon—when newlyweds were encouraged to drink *mead*, which was also called honey wine. People believed that mead increased sexual passion and encouraged fertility.

- The idea of taking a honeymoon trip originated in England in the 1800s when newly married aristocratic couples traveled throughout Europe for months. Commoners had neither the time nor the money to celebrate in this way; in fact, most people didn't even get a day off work for their wedding.

  By the early 20th century, couples in the United States started taking economical weekend honeymoon trips, the most popular destinations being the Pocono Mountains and Niagara Falls. It wasn't until the late 1940s and early 1950s that more people began to take longer honeymoons. The U.S. economy was booming, and Americans were eager to use their newfound discretionary income. In addition, it was during this time that employers began to offer paid vacation as a benefit to attract skilled workers, so a larger percentage of Americans could finally afford to take time off work.

- The average length of an American honeymoon today is seven days, and the average cost is $3,700.

- The top three honeymoon destinations for Americans are still domestic: Las Vegas, Hawaii, and the U.S. Virgin Islands.

Most Popular Pieces Recited at Weddings

1. I Corinthians chapter 13, from the Bible
2. The Song of Solomon, from the Bible
3. "Sonnet 116," by William Shakespeare
4. "How Do I Love Thee?" by Elizabeth Barrett Browning

The Language of Love

How to say "I love you"? Let us count the ways . . .

Afrikaans	"Ek het jou liefe."
Czech	"Miluji te."
Danish	"Jeg elsker dig."
Ethiopian	"Afgreki'."
Farsi/Persian	"Doostat daram."
Gaelic	"Ta gra agam ort."
Greek	"S'ayapo."
Hawaiian	"Aloha au ia 'oe."
Icelandic	"Eg elska thig."
Japanese	"Aishiteru."
Korean	"Sarang heyo."
Mandarin Chinese	"Wo ai ni."
Navaho	"Ayor anosh'ni."
Pig Latin	"Iay ovlay ouyay."
Swahili	"Naku penda."
Tahitian	"Ua here vau ia oe."
Yiddish	"Ikh hob dikh lib."

The Unfaithful Goddess of Love

Ancient Greek goddess Aphrodite really got around.

The Greeks believed Aphrodite to be the universe's most enchanting woman. She was born from sea foam and rose naked from the water on a scallop shell. When Zeus saw this spectacular specimen of feminine pulchritude, he whisked her off to Mount Olympus and declared her to be the goddess of love and beauty. But Zeus's wife, Hera, was jealous of Aphrodite and insisted that he marry her off to one of the other gods.

So Many Suitors, So Little Time

Many deities vied for Aphrodite's affections: Poseidon, god of the sea, offered to make her his queen, house her in a coral palace, and shower her with pearls and riches. Apollo (a multitalented god of medicine, music, and more) and Hermes, the messenger with winged feet, also wooed her. But Aphrodite remained detached and disinterested.

So Hera took the matchmaking into her own hands. She presented her son Hephaestus to Aphrodite. Hephaestus wasn't the best-looking fellow on Mount

Olympus, but he promised to give Aphrodite beautiful jewelry that would make her even more alluring. This appeal to her vanity won out, and Aphrodite accepted him. But she had no intention of being faithful. She reasoned that Hephaestus would be so busy tending to godly business that he wouldn't even notice her dalliances. She was wrong.

After discovering her affair with Ares, his brother and the god of war, Hephaestus divorced her. Aphrodite was back on the market, and other gods resumed their entreaties to her. Poseidon again pledged his interest, as did Dionysus, Ares, and Hermes. Each competed for her affections, and she had affairs with them all. But she never remarried.

Bad Dates: Something's Just Not Right

"We went to a Japanese steak house and had a great time. After we ate, we went back to my place, put in a movie, dimmed the lights, sat back, and started cuddling. After a few moments, we leaned closer and finally kissed. It couldn't get much better than that. But then something strange happened. She immediately pulled back, said "Uh-oh," ran to the bathroom, and threw up. I may not be the smartest man in the world, but after you kiss somebody, the first thing that should *not* happen is for her to get sick."

—*Matthew S.*

Lovers Through the Ages

When it comes to romance, the movies have nothing on real life.
From literature to science to sports and the Wild West,
here are some of history's greatest love stories.

Robert and Elizabeth Barrett Browning

Claim to Fame: Poets

First Meeting: Initially, theirs was an affair conducted in secret. Elizabeth Barrett was an invalid, the result of a childhood illness or injury (no one seems to be sure), and her life was strictly monitored by her controlling father. She was also a poet, not yet internationally famous but known in literary circles in England. A collection of her work entitled simply *Poems* was published in 1844 and gained her a fan in writer Robert Browning. Browning began sending her letters in 1845, first admiring her work and then admiring her. Over the next year, their correspondence turned into a love affair that they kept secret from Elizabeth's father, who disapproved of the relationship.

Life Together: In 1846, the pair eloped but still didn't tell Elizabeth's father right away. A week later, she and Robert moved to Italy, where they spent the next 15 years writing and raising a son. It was during this time that Elizabeth produced her most famous works: *Sonnets from the Portuguese* (1850), *Casa Guidi Windows* (1851), and *Aurora Leigh* (1857). She died in 1861, leaving her husband and son behind. But over the years, the story of the Brownings' love affair evolved into legend as Elizabeth, and later Robert (who gained commercial success with *Dramatis Personae* in 1864 and *The Ring and the Book* in 1868), became two of the most famous and popular poets of the 19th century. And Elizabeth's verse "How Do I Love Thee?" remains one of the most quoted poems in the world.

Annie Oakley and Frank Butler

Claim to Fame: Wild West superstars

First Meeting: Frank Butler was already an established Wild West show marksman when, in 1881, he bet an Ohio hotel owner that he could outshoot any local. The hotel owner took the bet ($100) and produced 21-year-old Annie Mosey as Frank's competition (Mosey didn't take the stage name "Oakley" until a couple of years later). The seasoned sharpshooter initially laughed at the hotelier's choice of a young girl but was quickly humbled by her skill. After Frank missed his final shot, Annie came away the winner, having hit all 25 of her marks. She also won his heart. Frank was captivated by both her independent personality and her tremendous skill with a pistol. The two struck up a friendship, then a courtship, and finally married in 1882.

Life Together: They immediately took their union on the

road. At first, it was Frank who was the traveling show star. Annie remained in the background until she got a lucky break: Frank's shooting partner didn't show up for a performance, so Annie stood in for him. She was such a hit with the crowd that Frank realized Annie, not he, had more star potential. They joined Buffalo Bill Cody's Wild West Show in 1885, and Annie quickly charmed audiences with her amazing tricks: she could shoot a dime thrown into the air and put six holes into a tossed playing card before it hit the ground. She and Frank also played up their relationship for laughs: in one act, she shot the ashes off of a cigarette Frank held in his mouth. As she became more of a star, Frank faded into the background, spending more time managing her career.

Frank Butler and Annie Oakley were married for 44 years. She died in November 1926, and he followed 18 days later. They were buried together at Brock Cemetery in Ohio.

For more historical love stories, turn to page 144.

"Love is the only thing that we can carry with us when we go."

—*Louisa May Alcott*

Puppy Love

*We asked some of the kids we know to define "love."
The answers they gave were remarkably wise.*

"Love is when two people like each a lot and then they get married. But if something goes wrong, they break up into little pieces."

—*Oliver T., age 5*

"I believe that love is two people caring about each other, and when you're old and loved, two people will die with each other."

—*Kaytlyn V., age 10*

"Love is when you would actually kiss someone, even your cat, your dog, your bird, or naked pet mole rat, not just your mom."

—*Connor N., age 6*

"When people see someone beautiful and they like them, they start dating and then they marry, and that means they love each other."

—*Duncan M., age 8*

"Love is when you give someone something like a hug or a heart."

—*Joshua B., age 4*

"Love means you care about your family and your friends and your dog and your horse. Love means everybody can go to school and the same dinner place." (Bailey's mom noted that she has been learning about Martin Luther King at school.)

—*Bailey T., age 5*

With age comes more perspective . . .

"Love is the journey of two soul mates to find their peace together. It is the soul completion of two beings. It brings joy, happiness, and care to the world."

—*Connor M., age 14*

Love

Love is something hard to explain
Love can be a pain
It can be forever
It unites humans together
to become one soul
Love can be sneaky
It can be out of control
as it brings humans together as a whole
Love is when you feel devotion towards someone
whether they feel it or not

—*Keegan M., age 12*

The Long and Short of Marriage

For some, it's a long haul—for others, a short ride.
Take a look at these marriage records.

Shortest Couple
Douglas Maistre Breger da Silva and Claudia Pereira Rocha married October 26, 1998, in Curitiba, Brazil. He's 35 inches tall; she's 36 inches.

Tallest Couple
The bride, Anna Swan, stood 7'5" tall (her hair was in an updo to give her an added inch or two); the groom, Martin Bates, measured 7'4". They met in New Jersey, when both were appearing in a traveling circus. The pair began performing together and soon fell in love. They married on June 17, 1871, in London.

Longest Marriage
The longest recorded marriage was 86 years. Liu Yang-wan from Taiwan married Liu Yung-yang in 1917. The marriage lasted until 2003 when Liu Yung-yang died at age 103; her husband was 104. The couple had more than 100 descendants by that time.

Longest (Combined) Wedding Ceremony

Once you add up all the times they've said their vows, this record goes to Lauren and David Blair. The couple was first married in 1984. Since that time, they have tied the knot in the United States, the United Kingdom, and the Dutch Antilles. In August 2006, they married each other for the 90th time at the Seaside Wedding Chapel in Myrtle Beach, South Carolina. When asked why they'd married so many times, David explained, "We love telling each other we love each other and looking into each other's eyes and saying our vows."

Shortest Celebrity Marriage

On January 5, 2004, Britney Spears and Jason Allen Alexander married in Las Vegas. The union lasted a whopping 55 hours before the couple got it annulled.

Longest Engagement

This "cold feet" award goes to Octavio Guillen and Adrian Martinez, who tied the knot in June 1969. By that time, they were both 82 and had been engaged since 1902.

Longest Wedding Dress Train

Norway's Hege Lorence wore a 670-foot silk train during her 1996 wedding to Rolf Rotset. Lorence enlisted 186 bridesmaids and page boys to help carry the train down the aisle.

"Love" on the Silver Screen

See if you can match the movie to its fun-fact clues.

A. *Love Me Tender* (1956)
B. *To Sir, With Love* (1967)
C. *Love Story* (1970)
D. *Love at First Bite* (1979)
E. *Shakespeare in Love* (1999)
F. *Love Actually* (2003)

1. Fun Facts

- This film's heroine actually misspoke its most famous line, which read "Love means not ever having to say you're sorry" in the original script.
- Michael Douglas, Jon Voight, Beau Bridges, and Peter Fonda all turned down the lead in this movie because they didn't think the film would be successful.
- Writer Erich Segal based this movie's main male character on Harvard students and roommates Al Gore and Tommy Lee Jones.

2. Fun Facts

- The title of this movie was originally *The Reno Brothers*.

- The title song from this movie is better known than the picture itself.

3. Fun Facts
- The person who plays the lead role in this film was the first African American actor to put his autograph, handprints, and footprints in the cement outside Grauman's Chinese Theatre in Hollywood.
- Although set and filmed primarily in England, this film was one of several groundbreaking stories about race relations that affected American audiences during the late 1960s.

4. Fun Facts
- In 2004, this was the most-rented DVD in the United Kingdom.
- One word (the second word in the film's title) is spoken 22 times by characters in the movie.
- This film's writer also penned (or co-penned) *Four Weddings and a Funeral, Notting Hill,* and *Bridget Jones's Diary.*

5. Fun Facts
- Julia Roberts, Winona Ryder, Daniel Day-Lewis, and Kenneth Branagh were all considered for this film's lead roles, but they didn't get the parts.

- One of this movie's actors won an Academy Award for her role in this film, though she was on-screen for only about six minutes.
- The American actress who plays the lead in this film is actually best known for playing British characters.

6. Fun Facts
- This movie spoofs a famous 1931 film.
- This movie also used the same makeup artist that the producers of that earlier film employed.
- The actor who stars in this film is the ex-father-in-law of both Angie Everhart and Shannen Doherty.

For answers, turn to page 175.

Longest Running "Wedding Ceremony"

Tony n' Tina's Wedding has been running off Broadway and in various cities around the United States since 1988. It's an interactive comedy, in which the audience members act as the "guests" at an Italian wedding ceremony and dinner reception. The audience mingles with the actors who play the bride, the groom, and their families and also enjoys an Italian buffet, a champagne toast, and dancing to a real wedding band.

Is That Lipstick on Your Collar?

Many women who wear no other makeup
wouldn't think of leaving the house without lipstick.
Here's a brief history of that paint you put on your lips.

- Anthropologists believe that early humans used lipstick to mark themselves as fertile. During sexual arousal, blood rushes to the lips and cheeks, so we naturally associate rosy lips and cheeks with healthy sexual appetites. Since procreation was essential for continuing human society and culture, it makes sense that humans found ways to enhance (or mimic) the signs of fertility.

- Both men and women in ancient Egypt painted their lips, but that lipstick was poisonous. The Egyptians used iodine, bromine, and a reddish-purple mercuric plant dye called fucus-algin to color their lips a deep ruby red. Effects of the concoction depended on exposure, but repeated use led to chronic intestinal problems and worse.

- During the 17th, 18th, and 19th centuries in England, lipstick (and makeup in general) was considered malevolent. Thomas Hall, a 17th-century English clergyman, believed that wearing makeup was satanic and that women who colored their lips did so to trap husbands and seduce men. Then, in 1770, the British passed a law saying that women who used lipstick and other makeup to lure men or trick them into marriage could be tried as witches. Finally, in the 19th century, Queen Victoria called all forms of makeup "impolite." She believed it should be worn only by actors and prostitutes (two of England's lowest classes).

- It wasn't until the early 20th century that lipstick became popular in the United States. During the World Wars, propaganda campaigns encouraged American women to "put on a happy face," both literally and figuratively. If they did things like paint their lips a cheery ruby red and send only happy letters to the front, their husbands and boyfriends could concentrate on the war effort and not worry about home and hearth. Cosmetic queen Elizabeth Arden even did her part to help out the World War II effort in the 1940s when she created a lipstick called "Montezuma Red." The lipstick was an effort to boost morale among women in the armed forces, and its color matched the red accents on their uniforms.

- Today, lipsticks are made with a mix of waxes, pigments, and oils, but some of the ingredients in modern lipstick will probably surprise wearers. Shimmery lipstick sometimes contains ground-up fish scales or mica, a mineral with sparkling properties. Natural dyes to produce the red coloring in lipstick often come from iron oxide—otherwise known as rust. And although it's expensive and therefore rarely used, a dye called carmine is sometimes included in lipsticks to make them bright red. Carmine is made from the crushed bodies of cochineal insects (a type of beetle). Think about *that* the next time you plant a big, wet one on your beloved!

Beauty Is Pain

Today, makeup sometimes takes a toll on a woman's wallet, but during the 16th century, it could be deadly. Queen Elizabeth and her contemporaries pioneered the snow-white skin look, and they used a face paint called Venetian ceruse to to achieve that pale countenance. But the makeup was a mixture of vinegar and white lead, which led to serious health problems. Many users got lead poisoning, which causes high blood pressure, kidney problems, and nerve disorders in adults. It also turns one's skin a sickly gray—not quite what they were hoping for.

Lovely Love Songs

*We polled the BRI to find some of the world's
most meaningful love songs. Then we tracked
down the stories behind those famous tunes.*

"Unchained Melody" (1955)

Lyrics by William Stirrat; music by Alex North

In 1936, 16-year-old William Stirrat was at an artsy
summer camp in Lake George, New York. Stirrat was
also head over heels for a girl named Mary Louise
Pierce, who lived back home in Schenectady, New York.
But he was too shy to tell her how he felt, so he spent
his time at camp writing lyrics for a song inspired by her.
When he finished, Stirrat asked Alex North, a composer
on the camp's staff, to write the song's music. "I pestered
him and pestered him," Stirrat recalled many years later;
finally, North conceded.

The song Stirrat wrote might have vanished if not for
North, who went on to write Hollywood film scores—
including those for *A Streetcar Named Desire* and *Death
of a Salesman*. In 1955, a producer hired North to score
a prison movie called *Unchained*. He remembered
Stirrat's tune (called "Unchained Melody"). The song,
he thought, could serve as the lament of the film's pris-
oner hero for his wife. The producers agreed and got

musician Les Baxter to perform it for the sound track.

That was the launching pad for one of the most-recorded songs of the 20th century. Four versions of "Unchained Melody" vied for space on the pop charts in 1955 alone; hundreds of other recordings followed. For many people, the 1965 Righteous Brothers version is the definitive rendition, but when the tune nabbed a 1955 Academy Award nomination for Best Song, Harry Belafonte performed it ("Unchained Melody" lost to "Love Is a Many-Splendored Thing").

"Ring of Fire" (1963)
Written by June Carter Cash

The love story of country music legends Johnny Cash and June Carter has been chronicled in numerous books, movies, and songs. One of the most famous versions involves the song "Ring of Fire." Johnny Cash scored a hit with this tune in 1963, but June penned the lyrics.

The pair spent their early years touring together but married to other people and trying to resist a love affair that ultimately consumed them. Johnny's drug addiction only compounded an already difficult situation. Of the song and the passionate early years that inspired it, June Carter Cash said, "['Ring of Fire'] was about Johnny Cash. I felt like I had fallen into a pit of fire, and I was literally burning alive." In the more than four decades since, "Ring of Fire" has been covered by many artists, including country singer Dwight Yoakam and rockers Coldplay and Social

Distortion. In 1999, June recorded it herself for the album *Press On*. But it's Johnny Cash's version, sung in his deep baritone and complemented by horns, that remains the best known. June Carter and Johnny Cash married in 1968 and remained so for more than 30 years. Both passed away in 2003, within just five months of each other.

"Something" (1969) and "Layla" (1970)

"Something" written by George Harrison
"Layla" written by Eric Clapton

Many rock wives play muse, but it's the rare one who inspires love songs by two guitar heroes. English model Patti Boyd, who was married to both George Harrison and Eric Clapton, holds that honor and is the woman for whom the songs "Something" and "Layla" were written.

Boyd met Harrison first, on the set of the Beatles' film *A Hard Day's Night* (in which she had a small role), and married him in 1966. Harrison began writing "Something" two years later and struggled with the lyrics, which, he said, just wouldn't come. He also fretted because the first line ("Something in the way she moves") was the same as that of a song by fellow musician and Beatles protégé James Taylor. Harrison put the song away for a time, but finally finished and released it in 1969. "Something" became one of the group's hits and the only Harrison-penned Beatles song to make it to number one. Frank Sinatra called it the greatest love song ever written.

Meanwhile, around this time, one of Harrison's friends,

guitarist Eric Clapton, had also fallen in love with Boyd. Clapton was so consumed with unrequited passion that he wrote the song "Layla" for her and released it in 1970. "Layla" was also a hit. In the end, Boyd left Harrison for Clapton, whom she married in 1979 (and divorced 10 years later). But the two musicians managed to stay friends throughout and even referred to each other as "husbands-in-law."

"The Rose" (1979)
Written by Amanda McBroom

In the mid-1970s, Amanda McBroom was an unknown songwriter living in Los Angeles. While driving one afternoon, she heard a song called "Magdalena" on the radio. One line caught her attention: "Your love is like a razor/My heart is just a scar." Initially, McBroom loved the lyric; it was clever, after all. But moments later, she realized she didn't agree with it, and that got her thinking: What is love, anyway?

As she continued toward home, lyrics flooded her brain, and she had to repeat them to herself so as not to forget them before she could write them down. When she arrived at home, she raced for her piano, wrote down the lyrics, and within minutes had written the song. She titled it "The Rose" and, a year later, offered it to a producer making a movie of the same name. The film's execs didn't like it; the gentle melody didn't fit the rock-and-roll project, they thought, so they rejected it. But the movie's star, Bette Midler, loved the ballad and insisted producers use it in the film. When the movie was released in 1979, it and its title song were huge hits; in 1980, both were nominated for Golden Globe Awards. The film lost, but McBroom's song took home a statue (so did Bette Midler, for Best Actress).

"Cowboy Take Me Away" (1999)
Written by Martie Maguire
In 1999, Dixie Chick Emily Erwin (soon to be Robison) was planning a wedding. Just a year before, she'd met singer Charlie Robison at a Dixie Chicks' show in Austin, Texas. The two hit it off immediately and, after only two months, decided to marry. Overjoyed by Emily's new romance, sister and fellow Chick Martie Maguire decided to write a song for the wedding. The tune she came up with was "Cowboy Take Me Away." Says Maguire, "It was inspired by my sister finding the love of her life. I always kind of worried about her, and I'm just so glad she found a good guy." The wedding took place in May 1999, and a year later, "Cowboy Take Me Away" reached number one on the music charts. It stayed there for three weeks and has become one of the band's signature tunes.

Nature's Singles Bar

*In their efforts to attract a mate, male animals will strut,
dance, and make any number of downright ridiculous
gestures to impress a receptive female. Here are some
of the strangest mating rituals in the animal kingdom.*

Doo-Doo You Love Me?

The male hippo has developed a form of foreplay that seems
to make him irresistible to the opposite sex. When the mood
strikes, he urinates and defecates simultaneously. Then he
uses his tail to stir up the mess and throw it about. Once he's
caught a female's attention, the pair proceeds to mate in
water (where, presumably, they will wash off).

Explosive Love

Mating is dangerous work for the male honeybee—when
he's done, he literally explodes. His body separates from
his genitals, which remain inside the female, preventing
her from mating with any other male.

Just Call Him Mommy

In a victory for women's liberation, sea horses have
reversed gender roles: the male sea horse gets "pregnant"
and nurtures the unborn young. Females use an organ

called an ovipositor to deliver her eggs into a male's body and impregnate him. Even better, sea horses mate for life and never cheat.

Cardinal Sins

Male Japanese cardinal fish nurture their immature young by incubating them in their mouths. But if a male encounters a female who is more desirable than his offspring's mother, the male fish quickly eats up all the babies and tries to woo the newcomer.

Won't You Come Up to My Place?

The male bowerbird of Australia and New Zealand builds an elaborate bachelor pad to entice a mate. He takes his time constructing the home, called a bower, with sticks and twigs and often decorates it with leaves, feathers, and dead insects. Female bowerbirds make the rounds of the various bowers before settling on a favorite. When a female chooses, the male launches into an energetic song-and-dance routine: he tosses feathers, runs around, and caws. All the trouble is worth it for the male; females often return year after year to the bower of a favorite male.

Lorena Bobbitt of the Animal World?

If an amorous male octopus approaches a female octopus who is not in the mood, she simply bites off his sex organ (fortunately, the male has seven others).

The (Complicated) History of Saint Valentine's Day

The course of true love never runs smooth, and neither does the history of Valentine's Day. Why do we celebrate romance on February 14? The answers are many.

Sentimental Saints

There were actually three saints named Valentine (a priest, a bishop, and a physician) who were, according to legend, all martyred in Rome on February 14, 270. Almost 200 years later, in 469, Pope Gelasius decided to give one of the Valentines a holiday: February 14. The pope wasn't clear, though, about which saint he meant to honor, so over time, the three men's stories merged, and two legends arose to explain Gelasius's decision.

Legend 1:

According to some, Valentine secretly performed marriages against the wishes of Roman emperor Claudius II. Claudius (who ruled from AD 268 to 270 and needed a powerful army to battle the invading Goths) thought single men were better soldiers than those who had wives and families. So he banned marriages in an effort keep his army strong. When the emperor learned that Valentine had continued to perform secret wedding ceremonies, he had the young priest executed.

Legend 2:
Another version is that, around AD 269, while in prison awaiting death for converting to Christianity, Valentine fell in love with the jailer's blind daughter and used his faith to restore her sight. Before his execution, Valentine wrote a good-bye note to his sweetheart and signed it "From Your Valentine."

Stories like these made Valentine a popular saint. But in 1969, the Church struck Saint Valentine's Day from its official calendar because Catholic researchers found it impossible to verify that Valentine actually existed.

Love's Lottery

Honoring a saint wasn't Gelasius's only motive for creating the holiday. By the time the pope officially introduced St. Valentine's Day, the Romans had been celebrating their own pagan holiday for at least 800 years. In ancient Rome, February was considered the beginning of spring—a time for birth and renewal. To usher in spring, the Romans participated in a mid-February fertility festival called Lupercalia.

Lupercalia honored Lupercus, the god of shepherds and agriculture. On the morning of February 15, Roman priests gathered at Lupercal, the cave where legend said a mother wolf raised Romulus and Remus, the founders of Rome. Priests sacrificed goats and gave the skins to Rome's young men, who cut the hides into strips called *februa*. Then the men ran around the boundary of the city and whipped young women with the februa, a ritual the Romans thought encouraged fertility. At Lupercalia, there was also a special lottery to honor Juno, the goddess of women and marriage. The names of available young women were put into an urn, and young men drew names for their partners at the festival, their lovers during the coming year, and maybe even their wives.

When Christianity came to power in Rome, however, the popes disapproved of all this heathen hanky-panky. So, in 469, Gelasius outlawed Lupercalia and gave the populace the holy day of St. Valentine in its place. According to some historians, the pope instituted a new lottery with young men drawing the names of saints, who would serve as their inspiration for the rest of the year.

Love Isn't Only for the Birds

Over time, the Lupercalia was forgotten, but so was the Church's "saintly" lottery. Men apparently preferred women to saints, and February 14 returned to its courtship roots. Around 500, the romantic aura of Valentine's Day was enhanced by the European belief that it was the time of year when birds mated. Centuries later, in 1377, English author Geoffrey Chaucer expressed this idea in his epic love poem titled "The Parliament of Fowls." Chaucer writes that, on Valentine's Day, "every fowl cometh there to choose his mate."

During this time, the custom of men giving women gifts also became associated with Valentine's Day. In 1415, Charles, Duke of Orleans, a Frenchman who had been captured in the Battle of Agincourt, wrote a Valentine's Day poem to his wife from his prison cell in the Tower of London. The Duke's poem is the oldest known valentine still in existence. And in 1668, English naval officer Samuel Pepys wrote in his diary (a book that became famous as a record of life in 17th-century London) of giving "his valentine" a guinea as a gift. By the end of the 1700s, written notes and love tokens were customary on Valentine's Day in both Europe and the United States.

The American Film Institute voted *Casablanca* to be the greatest movie love story of all time.

It's Symbolic

*Hearts and cupid are popular symbols of love, but
what else do people use to say "I love you"?*

Ghana and the Ivory Coast

Symbol: *Osram ne nsoroma*
Origin: This stenciled moon-and-star symbol represents
love and faithfulness; the feminine North Star awaits the
return of the masculine moon, her partner. The symbol
traditionally decorated textiles that priests used in religious ceremonies. Today, the *osram ne nsoroma* most often
appears on cloths used during wedding ceremonies and
other religious occasions.

China

Symbol: Lychee fruit
Origin: According to legend, an ancient Chinese emperor
fell in love with and married a woman who loved to eat
lychees, a sweet fruit that looks a little like a raspberry.
But because the fruit grows only in tropical areas and the
royals lived in northern China, the empress had trouble
keeping fresh lychees on hand. So her husband sent a
group of his fastest horsemen to southern China and had
them bring back the fruit so that his wife would have all

the fresh lychees she wanted. Because the emperor's actions showed such devotion for his wife, lychees came to represent love for the Chinese, and today the fruit is a popular gift between lovers.

Ireland

Symbol: The claddagh

Origin: This symbol typically appears on a ring and is made up of two hands holding a heart; a crown sits atop the heart. The two hands represent friendship; the crown, loyalty; and the heart, everlasting love. According to legend, the first claddagh rings appeared in the 17th century when pirates captured Richard Joyce (a fisherman from the town of Claddagh, Ireland, on the country's western shore), leaving Joyce's true love all alone. When Joyce was freed several years later, he returned to Ireland and married the woman he'd left behind. The two soon opened a goldsmith's shop. There, Joyce made the first claddagh ring for his wife. Soon after, the rings became popular with royalty in Great Britain; everyone from King Edward VII to Queen Victoria wore them. Today, they make popular gifts for lovers and friends worldwide.

Wales

Symbol: Love spoons

Origin: Romantic Welshmen can profess their love by offering hand-carved wooden spoons. The spoons originated during the 16th century among illiterate farmers who used the carvings—instead of words—to express their affection for the women they courted. The men usually used sycamore wood for the spoons and then carved ornate, symbolic designs: chained links symbolized loyalty and friendship, a diamond symbolized wealth, and an anchor meant that the carver had found a place where he wanted to settle with his beloved. In the old days, a man usually gave a love spoon to the woman he wanted to marry. Today, the spoons have general appeal and can be gifts at weddings, birthdays, or between friends.

Hawaii

Symbol: Leis

Origin: One of the ways people in Hawaii show their affection for each other is through the exchange of leis. This tradition dates back hundreds of years, to the first inhabitants of the Hawaiian Islands. Leis symbolize mercy and protection and are associated with the goddess Hiiaka, who represents those same qualities. Early Hawaiians gave leis to their royals as signs of affection or to enemies as peace offerings. Over time, commoners also began weaving and wearing leis. When European tourists started to visit the islands during the 1800s, leis became a welcoming symbol, offered up to make the outsiders feel comfortable. Today, leis encompass all of those senti- ments—affection, mercy, protection, and acceptance— and they're given during any ceremony in which "I love you" is a proper greeting.

Amore on the Airwaves

Television has given us some great fictional couples. Here are six of our favorites.

Ward and June, *Leave It to Beaver,* 1957–63

Before TV love got complicated, the Cleavers reigned supreme. Mom June (Barbara Billingsly) cooked up a storm; dad Ward (Hugh Beaumont) doled out sage advice to his sons Wally and Theodore (the Beaver). The Cleavers were one of TV's first popular families, and Ward and June were a "lovely" couple. The pair shared a room, but not a bed, so they usually showed their affection for each other in traditional, 1950s TV ways: June cooked hot meals, baked cakes, and gave her husband his nightly newspaper; Ward went to work and gently disciplined their children, making sure Wally and the Beaver treated their mother kindly and respectfully.

Gomez and Morticia, *The Addams Family,* 1964–66

In the 1960s, television expanded its scope to include all kinds of families: single parents (*The Andy Griffith Show*), orphans (*A Family Affair*), even witches (*Bewitched*'s

Samantha Stephens). But by far one of the most unique was the Addams family, headed by the ever-passionate Gomez (John Astin) and Morticia (Carolyn Jones). Some critics called Gomez and Morticia the era's most romantic TV couple. They certainly were attracted to one another: Morticia, a vamp with raven hair, often spoke French to her husband, something that drove him wild and inspired him to plant kisses up and down her arms. They were also surprisingly mainstream. Gomez and Morticia were dedicated to their family (Cousin Itt, Grandmama, and others were always visiting), were supportive in child rearing (both agreed it was strange for son Pugsley to join the Boy Scouts), and knew how to have fun together (they especially liked to fence with foils).

Sam and Diane, *Cheers*, 1982–93

Who could forget Sam Malone (Ted Danson) and Diane Chambers (Shelley Long)? She was a well-bred, well-educated graduate student; he was an ex–baseball player who owned a bar called Cheers. They met when she took a job as a waitress at the bar, and for the first season, they bickered and flirted like any good romantic TV couple. They got together in season two, broke up a year later, fought, dated other people, got back together, and finally got engaged in the fifth season. Then, just when *Cheers* fans thought Sam and Diane were really going to live happily ever after, Diane went off to write a book and didn't reappear at the bar until six years later. On her return, they teased fans with a fairy-tale ending, but in the series finale decided to part ways.

Cliff and Clair, *The Cosby Show*, 1984–92

Cliff (Bill Cosby) and Clair (Phylicia Rashad) Huxtable had one of the longest-standing and most functional relationships on television. He was an obstetrician who liked hoagies and potato chips. She was a tough but gentle attorney who monitored his unhealthy eating habits. Together they raised five children and three grandchildren and hosted friends and neighbors during the show's eight-year run. They weren't without controversy, however. Critics called the show an unrealistic portrayal of black families in America, arguing that the Huxtables' wealth, professional careers, and seemingly carefree lifestyle wasn't true to life and was an attempt to make African American characters palatable to white America. Supporters called that viewpoint inherently racist and lauded the show for putting an upper-class black family on television and allowing viewers to watch them go through the same trials and tribulations that affected families of any color. Through it all, the Huxtable parents respected and loved each other, supported their children, and gave America a sitcom family to be proud of.

David and Maddie, *Moonlighting*, 1985–89

They were detectives who loved each other, but apparently only the audience was aware of that fact. David

Addison (Bruce Willis) and Maddie Hayes (Cybill Shepherd) were clueless, making them one of the first TV couples to embody the foundation on which most modern TV couples have come to depend: sexual tension. He was a lovable jerk, she was an uptight former model, and for four seasons they swapped witty insults, witty banter, witty . . . well, everything, and left their audience wondering . . . and . . . wondering . . . and wondering, "When will these two get together?"

They finally did in season five, and then the show's ratings tanked. *Moonlighting* was canceled in May 1989. Was it because the characters finally admitted their feelings for one another, ruining the premise? Or did the 1988 Hollywood writer's strike, Cybill Shepherd's long maternity leave, and Bruce Willis's burgeoning film career have something to do with it? More than 15 years after the show left the air, debate continues among *Moonlighting* fans. But whatever the truth, the show did inspire a new showbiz term: many Hollywood TV producers continue to fear the dreaded "*Moonlighting* curse," that circumstance in which a show's main characters finally consummate their relationship . . . and doom their show to cancellation.

Ross and Rachel, *Friends*, 1994–2004

One of the best known and most often quoted television couples in history, Ross Geller (David Schwimmer) and Rachel Green (Jennifer Aniston) weathered their share of ups and downs during *Friends'* ten-year run. Fans, of course, knew they were destined to be together. Even the show's characters knew it—after all, he was her lobster. But after getting the characters together in season two, the writers decided to break them up the next year. For the next six seasons, Ross and Rachel got back together and broke up again, dated other people, got married, got divorced, and had a baby together. Then, finally, after ten seasons of angst, Ross and Rachel (and their fans) got their happy ending in the series finale when the two declared their love for each other and decided to stay together in New York. Awww.

Honorable Mention: Chandler and Joey, *Friends*, 1994–2004

They weren't technically a romantic pair, and yeah, Ross and Rachel got most of the press. But we all know that Joey Tribbiani (Matt LeBlanc) and Chandler Bing (Matthew Perry) were the greatest love story on *Friends*. They supported each other (remember how Chandler financed Joey's early acting career?), they had irrational fights (how about the time Joey squeezed himself into Chandler's entire wardrobe?), they went to extraordinary lengths to right wrongdoings (remember the episode when Chandler apologized for kissing Joey's girlfriend by spending hours in a box?), they had "children" together (the chick and the duck, of course), and they weren't shy about showing each other affection (has any television couple hugged more than they did?).

Marriage By the Numbers

*Facts and figures about the married
state (some blissful, some not).*

2
Number of times more likely husbands are to say they fell
in love with their wives at first sight than wives are to say
the same thing about their husbands

3 years
Age of a Nepalese boy who married a six-month-old girl in
2003. The ceremony was interrupted briefly when the
bride got a little fussy, but resumed after she and her
hubby-to-be were fed.

13 years
Minimum age at which girls in New Hampshire can marry
legally (the lowest age in the United States). Boys in New
Hampshire have to be at least 14.

17 percent
Newlyweds who say they consummated their relationship
on the first date

20 percent
Marriages around the world that are between first cousins

$25
Cost of a drive-through wedding ceremony at Las Vegas's Special Memory Wedding Chapel. The average cost of a traditional wedding in the United States is $27,000.

1,138
Federal U.S. benefits tied directly to marriage, including Social Security, inheritance rights, child custody, and immigration status, to name just a few

2,075
Couples married by Reverend Sun Myung Moon in a single ceremony on July 1, 1982, at Madison Square Garden in New York City. Most of the couples hadn't met until that day because Moon had arranged all of the marriages.

5,000
Approximate number of marriages between American men and foreign women that result every year from "mail-order bride" and e-mail correspondence services

55 million
Number of married households in the United States according to the 2000 census (another 5 million are unmarried-partner households)

The Original Book of Love

In the 1970s, The Joy of Sex *spent 11 weeks atop the*
New York Times *best-seller list. That pales in comparison
to the popularity of the* Kama Sutra, *which has been
educating lovers for more than 1,000 years.*

The *Kama Sutra* is a collection of drawings and about
800 verses that describe erotic practices and rituals.
The original version dates to between AD 100 and 500
and is attributed to Vatsyayana Mallanaga, a religious student and poet who lived in Pataliputra, India. He compiled a number of ancient writings (some that were attributed to associates of Hindu gods) to create the single
volume, originally called the *Vatsyayana Kamasutram*
("*Vatsyayana's Aphorisms on Love*"). It's a textbook of sorts,
compiled as a sexual etiquette manual to be used by upper-
class Indian bachelors in their struggle for fulfillment and
to aid them in finding a wife.

Censored!
More than 1,300 years passed before the *Kama Sutra*
reached the Western world. In 1883, Sir Richard Francis
Burton, a British linguist and explorer, oversaw the first
English translation. But Victorian England was a sexually
repressive society, so Burton's translation is much less

explicit than the original collection—the graphic sections (especially those describing genitalia) and ideas that clashed with Victorian morality (primarily discussions of female arousal) were removed.

Yet even with these edits, Burton's version was deemed pornographic, and the English government quickly banned the *Kama Sutra*. But not before 250 copies found their way into the hands of private collectors. (Very few are still around today, but a Massachusetts bookseller recently appraised one copy at $13,500.)

In 1963, Burton's edition was finally considered fit for public consumption and was reprinted. But it wasn't until 1994 that an accurate and unabridged translation by French historian Alain Daniélou, called *The Complete Kama Sutra*, hit bookstores.

What's Inside?

- The book contains 36 chapters, organized into seven parts: Introduction, Sexual Union, Acquisition of a Wife, Duties and Privileges of a Wife, Other Men's Wives, About Courtesans, and Attracting Others to One's Self. Part 2, with its chapters detailing sexual positions, is the best known but comprises only about 20 percent of the text.
- The *Kama Sutra* contains descriptions and illustrations for 64 sexual "postures," which include the armchair, the fusion, and the surprise. Lovers with back pain and arthritis are warned not to try some of the positions.

- There are also 64 "arts," or ways a woman can become a more refined lover and wife. These skills vary from the ordinary—singing, playing musical instruments, dancing, calligraphy, and cooking—to the unusual, such as distinguishing between true and false gems, being a master of disguise, teaching a bird to talk, making puns, and cheating at games.
- Indian men are supposed to marry virgins of their own caste, but they can have "relations" with women of a lower caste. These women fall into three categories: spinsters, remarried widows, and prostitutes/courtesans. Women proficient in the 64 arts are known as a *ganikas* (courtesans). They were originally highly sought after by upper-class Indian men and were compensated with money and expensive gifts.
- Males and females categorized into six physical types: man as rabbit (handsome and tender), bull (stout and earthy), or horse (sturdy and highly sexed); woman as deer (beautiful and soft-spoken), mare (slim and easily seduced), or she-elephant (gluttonous and highly sexed). According to the *Kama Sutra*, this allows for only three well-matched physical pairings that will result in a harmonious sexual relationship: rabbit/deer, bull/mare, and horse/elephant. The remaining couplings are thought to be disastrous for married couples.

Ring-a-Ding-Ding

Whether it's made of reeds, iron, or gold,
it's tough to say "I do" without a ring.

The wedding ring is the product of dozens of cultures and several centuries of marital evolution. The circle, always a symbol of eternity, has no beginning or end. So the ring was a natural symbol of the lasting union between a bride and groom. But the history of the wedding ring hasn't been all hearts and flowers.

It's the Money, Honey

Around 2800 BC in Egypt, money was molded as a ring. Ancient Egyptian marriage ceremonies involved placing the money on the bride's finger to show that she now possessed the wealth of the groom's family.

In ancient Rome, a similar custom evolved. Roman families kept wealth in strongboxes. New brides were given the keys to the strongboxes on a ring.

Christianity Comes A-Round

Oddly enough, many in the Christian church looked upon early wedding rings with contempt. Rings were seen as crude and pagan. It took a scandal before the early church gave wedding bands a ringing endorsement. The scandal arose because wedding rings could be made of hemp, reeds, or other cheap materials; worn-out rings were replaced every year or so. Eventually, shifty-eyed young men began presenting fair ladies with cheap rings and promises of eternal love, both of which fell apart quickly. Finally, the bishop of Salisbury published a law in 1217 saying that if a man gave a woman a ring in front of witnesses, it was a binding marriage contract. After the bishop laid down that law, most Christian sects embraced the wedding ring.

On the Rocks

Romans sealed matrimony with an iron ring (iron symbolized the strength of love), though they found that the iron rings rusted. Silver was popular for a time during the Renaissance, but eventually the English and Irish helped set the "gold standard." Folklore even suggested that a marriage could be deemed unlucky or legally invalid if the ring wasn't gold. If a couple couldn't afford a gold ring, somebody lent them one until after the ceremony.

When Archduke Maximilian I of Austria gave Mary of Burgundy a diamond engagement ring in 1477, diamonds became the wedding stone of choice. They symbolized luck, happiness, and magic. Ancient Greeks and Romans alike thought of diamonds as "tears of the gods." And a diamond's indestructibility is a fine symbol of

everlasting love. After 1870, the discovery of huge diamond caches in South America ensured that more grooms could afford to buy their sweeties diamond rings.

Love in Vein

In the 16th and 17th centuries, a fashionable woman might wear her wedding ring on her thumb. Later, it became popular to place the ring on the fourth finger of the bride's left hand—or the right hand, depending on what country you were from. A romantic legend concerning the left-hand tradition explains that the fourth finger of your left hand contains the *vena amoris*, which runs straight from your finger to your heart. (Alas for romantics, there's no scientific proof that the vena amoris exists.)

Three-Ring Circus

And we can't forget engagement rings. During the Middle Ages, *gimmal* rings were in vogue; a gimmal ring was a combination of two or three rings that could be worn as one ring or separated. One was given for engagement, the other was held by a witness, and the third was the wedding band.

In the 1700s and 1800s, gemstone "betrothal rings" were popular. They were sometimes crafted so that the first initials of the stones spelled out words. A ring for a Diane, for example, might have held a diamond, an iolite, an amethyst, a natrolite, and an emerald. But that fad passed (which was probably just as well for guys buying rings for an Elizabeth or a Chlothilde).

As for the groom's wedding ring, this custom of the 1900s is still in its infancy. The groom's ring may be a result of the 20th century's two world wars. A soldier shipped overseas had a ring to remind him of the loving wife waiting for him back home.

With This Ring

- Two months' salary is the spending guideline established by industry experts for an engagement ring. These experts, of course, sell engagement rings for a living.
- Among American brides, 74 percent receive a diamond engagement ring and 60 percent participate in the selection of their ring.
- The average cost of an engagement ring in the United States is $3,165.
- Saturday, the most popular day for a wedding in the United States, is, according to English folklore, the unluckiest day to marry!

Budget Be Damned!

*The average cost of a wedding gown for an American
bride today is between $800 and $1,500, but celebrity
brides aren't average. Their gowns are among the
most extravagant to make it down the aisle.*

Princess Diana

Probably the 20th century's most celebrated wedding was
Diana Spencer's 1981 marriage to England's Prince
Charles. More than 600,000 people packed the streets of
London to catch a glimpse of the wedding procession,
while another 750 million worldwide watched the ceremony on television. The bride did not disappoint. She
arrived by horse and carriage, wearing a silk ivory taffeta-
and-lace gown hand-embroidered with 10,000 pearls and
sequins and finished with a 25-foot-long train. The royal
family even had a spare wedding dress made for Diana
that looked a lot like the original but lacked the lace.
Diana wore the duplicate dress during early fittings (to
get the sizes right for the real thing), and in 2005 it sold
at auction for $180,000. The original is on display in
Great Britain at Althorp, Diana's family estate, now a
museum.

Grace Kelly

She was a movie star before she was a princess, so it's not surprising that Grace Kelly's 1956 wedding to Monaco's Prince Rainier III or the dress she chose for the occasion was extravagant. Helen Rose, an Oscar-winning costume designer who worked with Kelly in Hollywood, designed the silk ivory dress. It incorporated 98 yards of tulle, 25 yards of silk taffeta, and reams of 125-year-old lace; the veil was embroidered with orange blossoms and pearls. MGM gave Kelly the $8,000 dress and veil as a wedding gift, and after the ceremony, the royal couple donated the dress to the Philadelphia Museum of Art (in Grace Kelly's hometown). It remains on display there today.

The day before the public ceremony, Grace Kelly and Prince Rainer had a private civil wedding ceremony, a requirement for marriage in Monaco. Again, Kelly's dress fit the affair, though this time the tone was more classical. She wore a beige lace dress and a matching hat.

Sarah Salleh

In September 2004, Sarah Salleh, a 17-year-old commoner, married Brunei's Crown Prince Al-Muhtadee Billah Bolkiah, and the outfit she wore to her wedding was fit for royalty. The bride arrived at the ceremony (held in the royal family's 1,788-room main palace) wearing a hand-embroidered blue silk dress and veil. She also donned a diamond-studded tiara and diamond-studded shoes, and carried a gold and diamond bouquet (flowers, it seems, just weren't fancy enough). After the nuptials had been exchanged, Salleh and Bolkiah climbed into a gold Rolls Royce limousine that took them to their reception. Their guests included Saudi Arabia's Prince Bandar, the prime minister of Singapore, and Japan's Crown Prince Naruhito.

Melania Trump

In January 2005, Donald Trump and Slovenian model Melania Knauss tied the knot in Palm Beach, Florida. And even though both claimed to want a small ceremony (it was Trump's third marriage, after all), they ended up with a guest list that included more than 350 people. One of the day's highlights was Melania in a $200,000 Christian Dior gown. The dress was made of white satin, was embroidered with 1,500 crystals and pearls (a job that took 550 hours to complete), had a 13-foot train, and weighed 50 pounds!

From Valentines, with Love

Living in a place called Valentines inspired Willie Wright to start a tradition that gave lovers around the country a reason to appreciate an otherwise insignificant dot on Virginia's state map.

The year was 1951. Willie Wright was just 21 years old, and he'd become postmaster of Valentines, Virginia (population 85). The post office itself wasn't much to speak of; it didn't even have its own building and instead occupied one corner of the town's general store.

Each year, around Valentine's Day, Willie's post office received numerous requests from people who wanted a Valentines postmark on their cards. Willie always obliged, and in 1956, he designed a Valentine's-themed rubber stamp to be used with the Valentines, Virginia, postmark cancellation. The stamp was comprised of a heart and dogwood flowers—the dogwood is Virginia's state flower—and included the words "With Love. . ." (all in red, of course). Willie mostly used the stamp during the Valentine season, but he also broke it out for special occasions . . . when a stack of wedding invitations came his way, for instance.

Valentines from Valentines

Soon, word got out about Willie's stamp, and romantics everywhere wanted their sentimental missives adorned with the Valentines postmark and stamp. Each year, as Valentine's Day approached, cards arrived at Willie's post office, accompanied by requests that each one be hand-canceled and remailed. At first, people learned of the opportunity by word of mouth, but as the years went by, reporters and other media told the story. A national television report in 1984 catapulted the requests to more than 25,000 cards and letters. Four years later, the number had grown to 88,000 valentines.

It was a lot of work, but Willie's wife Frances, who doubled as the relief postmaster, helped out. In the early years, the Wrights stamped the letters themselves, even during peak season (a four-week period from mid-January through Valentine's Day). But as the years passed and the number of letters increased, the Wright children lent a hand, and postal workers from neighboring towns volunteered their time. One person opened the large envelopes, another sorted the mail, another stamped the envelopes, and yet another canceled each letter.

A Labor of Love

By the time he retired in 1999, Willie Wright had made Valentines, Virginia, famous—and not just for his stamp. Every February, Willie and Frances decorated the post office for Valentine's Day, and thousands of people stopped by to see it. Couples got married on the steps of the store or at the post office window. Newspaper reporters, magazines, television stations, and even Dear Abby recorded it all. And on February 1, 1995, the U.S. Postal Service honored Willie by choosing his post office to unveil its Love cherub stamp.

Willie Wright died in June 2006, but his passing didn't end his legacy of love. Valentines' new postmasters continue the envelope-stamping tradition. And the post office is still swamped in the weeks before Valentine's Day. Lovers who want to send a hand-canceled letter from the post office need only to mail their prestamped, preaddressed envelopes inside a large envelope to Postmaster, Valentine Re-mailing, Valentines, VA 23887.

What's in a Name?

Valentines, Virginia, got its name not in the spirit of romance but from businessman William H. Valentine, who opened the town's first store and post office in 1887, the same place where Willie Wright started using his Valentines stamp almost 70 years later.

The Saga of
Abélard and Héloise

*Life's funny. One day you've got the world on a string—a beautiful
lover, a successful career. The next day, well, you wouldn't wish
Peter Abélard's next day on your worst enemy.*

Toward the end of the Middle Ages, the Catholic
Church ran pretty much everything in Europe. If you
wanted to study, you went to a monastery—that's where
the books were. If you wanted to learn, you went to the
priests—that's who the teachers were.

Our Hero

Take Peter Abélard, a cleric and popular teacher in
France during the 12th century. (The group of students
who gathered to hear him speak eventually evolved into
the University of Paris.) The Catholic Church's clerics
weren't priests, but they had to follow some of the same
rules—like celibacy. Abélard, in his late 30s, ran afoul of
this particular rule when he seduced his landlord's niece,
17-year-old Héloise, who was known for her brilliant
mind and beauty.

Héloise's guardian, her uncle Fulbert, had a room to
rent, and Abélard needed a place to stay. A few months

later, Fulbert caught the couple in bed and threw Abélard out of his house.

Teenage Runaway

But by then, Héloise was pregnant. She managed to get word to Abélard, who helped her sneak away to live with his relatives. Héloise gave birth to a son she named Astrolabe, and then she returned to Paris, content to remain Abélard's lover; she didn't want to get married. Fulbert insisted on a wedding, but marriage would have ended Abélard's career as a teacher and philosopher because a married man couldn't be part of the Catholic Church's hierarchy.

Abélard's compromise was to marry Héloise but to keep the marriage secret, which didn't satisfy Uncle Fulbert. What good was a secret marriage in restoring family honor? The furious Fulbert got revenge in the worst possible way. He hired a gang of thugs to castrate Abélard.

Picking Up the Pieces

Justice in those days was swift and vengeful. The thugs were caught, tried, then blinded and castrated themselves. Uncle Fulbert got off lightly; all he lost was his property. Now that celibacy wasn't an issue for Abélard, he joined a monastery and became a full-fledged priest. Héloise became a nun. Both withdrew from city life to live in religious communities, and they probably never saw each other again. We know about their love story, their accomplishments, and even about their wild exploits (like the

time they made love in a convent's dining room) from
their letters. Some of the letters, oozing with passion and
sadness, were written to each other; others went to friends.
You can read them, too, if you want—they're still being
published today.

Rebel to the Bitter End

In academic circles, Abélard's real claim to fame was that
he used confrontation and questions to make his students
think. This was unusual in the 12th century, when few
people dared to question the Church. Abelard kept up his
rebellion, however, and one of his books actually listed
contradictions between the Bible and Church authorities.
He hoped to teach his students that, by using careful ques-
tioning, they could reach the truth. The Church found his
teachings so blasphemous that Abélard was forced to burn
his own book. But he kept writing and teaching . . . and
making enemies. Finally he was labeled a heretic. More
books were burned, and the pope condemned Abélard to
silence—sheer torture for him. The sentence was lifted
before long, but Abélard was old and ill by then; he died
on the way to Rome, hoping to explain his methods to the
pope directly.

Héloise lived for 20 years after Abélard's death and
became an abbess. She corresponded with many of the
famous men of the day—even some of Abélard's old enemies. When she died, she was buried beside Abélard at a
convent in northeastern France.

Make-Out Songs

*Can you match the romantic songs with
the artists who made them famous?*

1. His baby's got blue eyes, which apparently laugh in the
sun and rain—so maybe his baby doesn't wear outrageous
sunglasses like he does. Who wrote and performed "Blue
Eyes"?
   A. Louis Armstrong
   B. Elton John
   C. Sting
   D. Barry Manilow

2. Priscilla couldn't help it, and millions of screaming
1950s teens couldn't either. Who made "Can't Help
Falling in Love" famous the first time around?
   A. Frankie Avalon
   B. Andy Williams
   C. Elvis Presley
   D. Davy Jones

3. He explored the seasons on Jupiter and Mars and
begged his lover to be true in "Fly Me to the Moon." Who
is this famous crooner?

A. Dean Martin
B. Perry Como
C. Tony Bennett
D. Frank Sinatra

4. The daughter of this band's lead singer made out to this very song—and didn't close her eyes—in the movie *Armageddon*. Which rock band recorded "I Don't Want to Miss a Thing"?
   A. KISS
   B. Aerosmith
   C. Guns N' Roses
   D. AC/DC

5. Dolly Parton wrote the song "I Will Always Love You," which became the soundtrack to the movie *The Bodyguard*, starring this pop star diva, who subsequently recorded it. Who is she?
   A. Mariah Carey
   B. Jessica Simpson
   C. Whitney Houston
   D. Céline Dion

6. It helps to relieve his mind, and it's good for him—or so the song "Sexual Healing" proclaims. What soul great recorded this racy hit?
   A. Marvin Gaye
   B. James Brown

C. Luther Vandross

D. Al Green

7. Stay away from his window, and stay away from his back door, too—this 1970s and '80s rock icon proclaims, "Tonight's the Night."

    A. Mick Jagger

    B. Rod Stewart

    C. Eric Clapton

    D. David Bowie

8. The first nine words of this song are "love," and the song repeats the word at least several dozen times before it fades out. Which band made "All You Need Is Love" popular in the late 1960s?

    A. Rolling Stones

    B. Bee Gees

    C. Beatles

    D. Herman's Hermits

9. Too much is never enough for this Motown artist, who proclaims he's insatiable in "Can't Get Enough of Your Love."

    A. Lionel Richie

    B. Michael Jackson

    C. Stevie Wonder

    D. Barry White

10. In 1975, in discos around the country, everyone was in a spin over "Love to Love You, Baby," sung by what sultry queen of disco?

   A. Chaka Khan
   B. Cher
   C. Donna Summer
   D. Aretha Franklin

For answers, turn to page 175.

Rings of the Stars

- Before acquiring fame and fortune, Sonny and Cher were wed with engraved $10 stainless steel rings. Cher lost hers. But 26 years later, shortly after Sonny Bono's death, a construction worker found the ring and returned it to Cher, after hearing her talk about it on Jay Leno's TV show.
- Actors David Arquette and Courteney Cox Arquette have "A Deal's a Deal" engraved inside their wedding rings.
- Jennifer Lopez lost a wedding ring while filming *Gigli*. The ring's cost? More than $30,000. Nobody owned up to seeing it—sort of like *Gigli* itself.
- England's Queen Victoria gave out more than 50 rings at her wedding.

Together in the Taj

*It took two decades to build, but the jeweled and sparkling
Taj Mahal has stood for more than 350 years as an
enduring symbol of commitment and love.*

In 1607, 15-year-old Khurram, son of India's emperor
Jahangir and a descendant of Ghengis Khan, strolled
through a bazaar in Agra, India, and saw a girl selling glass
beads. She was 14-year-old Arjumand Banu Begum, beautiful granddaughter of the emperor's chief advisor. It was
love at first sight, and Khurram vowed to take Arjumand
as his bride.

Khurram had to wait, however. In those days, an Indian
prince (who was allowed four wives) was duty-bound to
marry whomever his father ordered. Emperor Jahangir
agreed to the betrothal of Khurram and Arjumand, but first
the prince had to marry a well-connected Persian princess
who brought powerful royal alliances to the family.

Together in War and Peace
Khurram acquiesced, but he never forgot Arjumand. For
five years he waited, unable to marry her yet having the
permission. They weren't allowed to see each other during
this period, and that only increased their desire to be
together.

Finally, in 1612, Khurram was allowed to marry Arjumand. The ceremony was elaborate. Dancers, acrobats, and trained animals entertained the attendees. The emperor himself threw a feast in the couple's honor, a rarity for Indian royalty at the time.

The new husband and wife were inseparable. To keep control over his kingdom, Emperor Jahangir often sent his son to the far reaches of the empire. Arjumand always went along on these military assignments, forsaking the ease of the palace and traveling with Khurram, even when she was pregnant—Arjumand and Khurram had 14 children, seven of whom survived.

When Emperor Jahangir grew ill, a civil war broke out among Khurram and his brothers over succession; Khurram, a skilled warrior, emerged victorious. In 1628, he ascended the throne as Emperor Shah Jahan, a name that translates to "king of the world." At his side was his beloved Arjumand, on whom he bestowed the name Queen Mumtaz Mahal, meaning "chosen one of the palace."

A Generous Queen

Shah Jahan trusted his queen implicitly. He allowed her to use his imperial seal and to conduct affairs of state. She had a reputation for gentleness and was a

generous, compassionate royal. On her husband's ascension to the throne, she distributed jewels and gold to the country's poor. She also paid dowries for girls whose families couldn't afford them and even convinced her husband to save the lives of criminals scheduled to be executed.

Three years later, in 1631, Shah Jahan was quelling a rebellion in southern India when Mumtaz Mahal got sick. The queen was in labor with their fourteenth child when complications arose. Shah Jahan rushed to his wife's side, but she was dying. The queen asked her husband to build her a tomb that would serve as a lasting symbol of their love.

Building the Tomb

Shah Jahan's grief for his deceased wife was so intense that he plunged his entire court into two years of mourning. Playing music, wearing bright colored clothes, and wearing jewelry and perfume were forbidden; anyone who disobeyed was executed. The king himself exchanged his elaborate royal cape for white mourning clothes. Shah Jahan also lost interest in governmental affairs and focused only on fulfilling his promise to his queen.

He hired more than 22,000 workmen to create the tomb. Shah Jahan devoted the next 20 years of his life and more than 32 million rupees (much of his treasury) to build the structure. He chose a spot for the tomb beside the banks of the Yamuna River. Fleets of elephants hauled in Makrana marble from quarries around India. Gemstones from Tibet, China, Afghanistan, and other countries adorned the structure's walls. Builders created designs of inlaid jasper, onyx, agate, jade, crystal, and turquoise. These floral and geometric designs were so intricate that nearly 50 stones might be used in just one square inch of decoration.

The tomb was completed in 1652, and it became known as the Taj Mahal (or "crown palace"). Its mausoleum, gardens, reflecting pools, tomb, mosque, and minarets are considered among the finest Mughal (Islamic, Persian, and Indian) architecture in the world.

Five years after its completion, Shah Jahan fell ill, and his own family began warring over the right to rule the empire. His son Prince Aurangzeb won the throne, deposed his father, and imprisoned the ailing king at a fort in Agra. There, Shah Jahan could look through the windows and see the Taj Mahal gleaming on the other side of the river. In 1666, he died, and Aurangzeb had him entombed in the Taj Mahal beside his beloved queen.

The oldest love poem dates from 4000 BC. It was composed on a clay tablet and addressed to Shu-sin, king of the Sumerians (the culture that also invented writing). No one knows who wrote the poem or its title, but the scientists who found it gave it the unromantic name of "Istanbul #2461."

I Thee Wed

Ah, marriage, that sacred institution.

Imagine the Honeymoon!

In June 1998, Janet Downes married her "perfect" mate . . .
herself. The Nebraska native (who also turned 40 the day
of the wedding) said she wanted to celebrate the fact that
she was "happy with [herself]." She wore black to the wedding; had a cake, music ("My Way," of course), and flowers; and recited the vow, "I, Janet Downes, take myself
with all my strengths and faults . . ." in front of a mirror.

You Drive Me Crazy, Baby

A Knoxville, Tennessee, man tried
to marry his car in 1999. He
showed up at the courthouse,
paperwork in hand—he even
listed the Mustang's birthplace
as Detroit, father "Henry Ford,"
and blood type "10-W-40"—
and applied for a marriage
license. The application was
rejected, but . . . good try!

A Dog's Life

Canadian pooches Jigger and Malika tied the knot in 2003. Some of the prewedding festivities were a bachelor party for Jigger that included a stripper (a female pug in a bikini) and a spa day for Malika. Then, on the big day, the bride wore a doggie dress embroidered with 1,000 beads, an ordained minister presided over the affair, and more than 30 canine guests were in attendance.

How Charming

Bimbala Das, a 30-year-old Indian woman, married a cobra in 2006. The snake lived in an anthill in Orissa state; the woman, in a nearby village. The bride and 2,000 guests attended the ceremony, but the groom was MIA. A snake charmer tried to coax him out of his underground home, but the effort was unsuccessful, so a gold snake statue acted as a stand-in. The bride wore a traditional silk sari, and Hindu priests chanted the vows. After the ceremony, Das moved into a hut near the anthill . . . presumably so she could be closer to her new husband.

The *London Times* reported in February 1840 that Queen Victoria's wedding cake was more than nine feet in diameter.

More Lovers
Through the Ages

*Our look at history's great romances concludes with
two inspirational stories. (Part 1 is on page 84.)*

(Part 1 is on page 84.)

Marie and Pierre Curie

Claim to Fame: Scientists extraordinaire

First Meeting: French scientist Pierre Curie had all but
given up on finding a wife. The women he met showed no
interest in science, and he wanted a partner who was as
passionate about science, research, and discovery as he
was. He found her in the form of a Polish immigrant
named Maria (later Marie) Sklodowska. Marie came to
Paris in 1891 to study physics and received her first master's degree two years later. She met Pierre in 1894 when a
professor friend suggested that she use a room in Pierre's
laboratory as a research space for her doctoral studies.
Marie and Pierre hit it off immediately, and they loved science with equal fervor.

Life Together: The two married in 1894, though neither
wanted rings or a religious wedding. In fact, at their civil
marriage ceremony, Marie wore a dark blue outfit that
later also served as her laboratory uniform.

Over the years, the Curies had two daughters (Irène in 1897 and Ève in 1904) and solidified one of the most famous and successful scientific partnerships in history. They discovered two new elements (radium and polonium), pioneered radiology, and introduced the world to the term "radioactivity." They also won the 1903 Nobel Prize in Physics and did research together until Pierre's sudden death in 1906. He was killed after being hit by a carriage, and Marie was devastated. But she continued to study for the rest of her life. She took over Pierre's teaching post at the Sorbonne after his death, the first woman to hold such a position, and won another Nobel Prize in 1911, this time for chemistry.

Marie Curie died in 1934 of leukemia, probably the result of years of exposure to radium and radioactive material. But the Curies' children and grandchildren carried on their scientific legacy. Irène Curie and her husband Frédéric Joliot received the Nobel Prize in Chemistry in 1935. Irène's son Pierre Joliot is a biophysicist, and daughter Hélène Langevin-Joliot, a nuclear physicist. Hélène's son Yves Langevin is an astrophysicist.

Jackie and Rachel Robinson

Claim to Fame: Sports heroics and civil rights activism
First Meeting: Jackie Robinson met Rachel Isum in 1940 when both were students at UCLA. He was already a college baseball star, and she was a first-year nursing student. They seemed an unlikely pair, but for the next six years

their romance blossomed, and they finally married in 1946. Two weeks later, the Robinsons boarded an airplane bound for Florida. Jackie was headed to spring training and would soon become the first African American to play for a 20th century major league baseball team—he joined the Brooklyn Dodgers in 1947 and led them to a 1955 World Series win. Always cheering him on was Rachel.

Life Together: Being the first black major league player was tough. During that first spring training camp and the subsequent year Jackie spent on the Dodgers' minor league team, he suffered death threats, insults, and beanballs thrown at his head. It was Southern racism at its worst, the likes of which neither Jackie nor Rachel had experienced before, as both spent most of their early lives in California. Through it all, though, the Robinsons remained committed to each other and to Jackie's career. When he moved up to the major leagues, the racism got worse . . . and the couple's relationship got stronger. Jackie once told a magazine reporter, "When they try to destroy me, it's Rachel who keeps me sane."

Jackie Robinson retired from baseball in 1956, but he and Rachel remained in the public eye, staying committed to civil rights and integration. The couple supported Martin Luther King Jr. but denounced Stokely Carmichael and other black separatists. The Robinsons also had three children—Sharon, David, and Jackie Jr. Says Sharon Robinson, "[My mother] was in a real partnership with my father. We felt that. We knew that."

Jackie Robinson died on October 23, 1972, from a heart attack. Rachel continued to support her husband's legacy and civil rights work. In 1973, she created the Jackie Robinson Foundation, which helps send minority students to college, and she served as the organization's chair until she retired in 1996.

This Spud's for You

In 2006, during national Potato Lover's Month (February, for those not in the know), a heart-shaped potato ended up on the kitchen table of Pennsylvanian Linda Greene. Greene claims to love all things heart-shaped, so she saved the potato. When the Idaho Potato Commission found out about the misshapen spud, officials explained that such unique shapes are usually saved for processed foods (dehydrated potatoes and French fries). In this case, said commission president Frank Muir, an inspector must have noticed the potato's fun shape and decided to put it through to the public. Although some people wondered if the commission had planned the whole thing as a public relations ploy, Muir assured the media that was not the case. For her part, Greene couldn't help wondering if she could plant her potato and grow a garden of heart-shaped spuds.

Making Scents

From ancient Egypt through the French Revolution to modern times,
women (and men) have used perfume to indulge their senses.

The Egyptians: Keeping It Practical

The ancient Egyptians were the first people to use perfumed oils. Archaeologists have found alabaster jars containing trace amounts of perfume buried with pharaohs and wealthy commoners. The Egyptians mostly used the sweet scents to mask body odor. Women in particular wore rose, orange blossom, and other flower essences to deodorize themselves. And Queen Cleopatra treated herself to a daily rubdown with henna, olive oil, and jasmine oil.

Perfumes in ancient Egypt were also used as embalming agents. Herbal resins and oils worked both as preservatives on cadavers and as natural deodorants for the dearly departed.

The Greeks: Making Perfume Popular

The ancient Greeks viewed perfume as a luxury and applied it daily. They sprinkled floors with perfume, rubbed themselves down with it before athletic endeavors, and used scents as part of ritual cleansings. They even designed specific scents for different body parts: rose water on their arms and hands, orange blossom oil on their heads, and rosemary on their feet. Perfumes made of lavender, rosemary, and other herbs were also used as medicines for both physical and mental ailments.

During formal banquets, the Greeks purified their hands: an attendant poured perfumed oil over a diner's fingers to clean and scent them. Servants regularly sprinkled the diners with expensive perfumes, and white doves whose wings were saturated with oils flew over the banquet table—the scents wafted down from their wings and further perfumed the festivities. After dinner, the Greeks scented their breath with a drink called "myrrhinne," a combination of myrrh, honey, flower oils, and wine.

Not everyone in ancient Greece appreciated the ubiquity of perfumes, though. Solon, an Athenian lawmaker who ruled around 600 BC, was disgusted by the culture's apparent addiction to perfume, and he passed a law that forbade anyone from selling it. This decree was wildly unpopular, so the Greeks ignored it and continued to revel in their scents.

Early French: Secret Scents

When we think of expensive fragrances, we typically think of France and its lavish perfume industry. French queen Catherine de Medici, who reigned during the 16th century, introduced her court to the first French perfumes. Catherine employed a private perfumer, René le Florentin, who kept her supplied with fragrances—two of the most popular included valerian, an earthy-smelling herb reminiscent of animals, and musk oil, glandular secretions from a musk deer. Florentin mixed these with waxes, oils, and other ingredients to create a kind of fragrant pomade. To protect this precious stash, Catherine provided Florentin with a special apartment connected to her bedroom via a secret passageway. Florentin used this passageway when delivering his formulas to the queen so that none of her signature scents could be stolen en route to her chamber.

Later French: Perfume and Gloves

Nearly a century later, perfumed gloves became the fashion for wealthy folks in France. Perfumers rubbed scented oil into the gloves' leather; the oil was then absorbed into the skin of the wearer—who enjoyed the fragrance even after removing the gloves. Common scents used in gloves included citrus, ginger, rose, lavender, and musk.

Glove making was an influential industry during this period, and in 1656, the Guild of Glove and Perfume Makers was established so that the glove makers kept a monopoly on scent manufacturing. Thus, the first commercial perfumers in France were known as *les maitres gantiers* (masters in glove making). By law, only guild members were allowed to make and sell perfume. This law remained in effect until the 18th century, when perfumed gloves went out of style and the perfume industry took off on its own, primarily in southern France, where the climate was ideal for growing the flowers and herbs used to make perfume. The village of Grasse in Provence became (and remains) the country's perfume capital. Chemists at perfumeries there experimented with different scent formulas, and soon the perfumes were renowned throughout the world for their quality and complexity. Today, perfume plants in Grasse manufacture more than 50 percent of all French perfumes.

In the early 19th century, musk perfumes from Grasse were especially popular. Manufacturers there found ways of making the scent smell stronger and last longer than before. These musks gained popularity among the French elite; even Emperor Napoléon's first wife, Josephine, was a fan. She used musk scents to such excess that servants in her bedroom sometimes fainted from an overdose of the perfume.

Modern Perfumes: Diamonds and Dollars

Today, perfume is an $8-billion-a-year business. The French perfume industry remains strong, but American manufacturers now capture 60 percent of the market. French women, however, remain more dedicated to perfumes than their American counterparts: approximately 75 percent of American women wear perfume daily, compared to 90 percent of French women.

Modern women—and men—have myriad perfumes from which to choose. More than 10,000 scents flood the market worldwide, and more than 200 new ones are launched each year. The two most popular—each capturing 5 percent of the perfume market—are the classic Chanel No. 5 (launched in 1921) and the relative newcomer CK One, a unisex scent launched in 1994 by Calvin Klein.

The high cost of perfume still makes it a luxury. Although some low-cost scents sell for $10 to $20 an ounce, fine perfumes made with expensive ingredients and carrying trendy brand names can go for hundreds of dollars or more an ounce. The most expensive is Imperial Majesty by London's Clive Christian Company. The perfume costs as much as $2,000 an ounce and also holds the record for coming in the most expensive perfume bottle. For about $200,000, purchasers of the limited-edition bottles sold in 2005 acquired an ounce of Imperial Majesty in a Baccarat crystal flask decorated with a five-carat diamond.

Quote Me Again

"The heart is a free and fetterless thing—a wave of the ocean, a bird on a wing."

—*Julia Pardoe, English writer*

"All the knowledge I possess, everyone else can acquire. But my heart is all my own."

—*Goethe*

Starry, Starry Night

A heavenly love story creates an Asian holiday.

Every year, the Chinese and Japanese cultures celebrate the Night of the Sevens (called Qi Xi in China and Tanabata in Japan). The holiday's actual date often varies depending on the year—it takes place on the seventh day of the seventh lunar month on the Chinese calendar (usually in July or August)—and its details vary depending on the culture. But the basic story remains the same.

The Weaver and the Cowherd

In the Chinese version, a cowherd named Niulang (who represented the star Altair) saw seven fairies swimming in a lake. Being a trickster, he stole their clothes. When the youngest fairy, a beautiful weaver girl named Zhinu (the star Vega) who made clouds for the sky, came looking for her clothes, Niulang saw her naked, and the two had to marry.

They soon fell in love, but the goddess of heaven was angry that an ethereal girl had married a mortal. So the goddess created a wide river of stars in the sky (the Milky Way) to keep them apart. Niulang and Zhinu were devastated and pined for each other from their places in different parts of the sky. So once a year (on the seventh day of the seventh lunar month), the world's magpies would fly up to heaven and create a bridge so the lovers could reunite. This period of the year is also the time when the Milky Way dims and the stars Altair and Vega, which are usually separated, appear together in the night sky.

The Japanese story has some variations: Instead of the goddess of heaven separating the lovers, it's an emperor named Tentei, the weaver's father and the ruler of the heavens. And instead of magpies, Tentei hires a boatman to carry his daughter across the Milky Way once a year.

Modern Celebration

Men and women in Asia have been celebrating this holiday together for more than 2,000 years. And even though its origins are in China, it has become more associated with Japan, where elaborate celebrations take place every year. The largest and most well known are in Tokyo in July and the city of Sendai in August. During these festivals, people decorate their homes and businesses with long, colorful streamers, lovers exchange gifts, there are parades and carnival games, townspeople light lanterns and float them in streams and rivers, and some places even crown a Miss Tanabata. Japanese women also wear *yukatas* (special diaphanous kimonos) on Tanabata, and celebrants write wishes on bits of paper that they then hang on bamboo trees; legend holds that the lovers (named Orihime and Hikoboshi in Japan) will grant these wishes.

Proverbial Love

*Some advice for lovers from around the
world . . . take it with a grain of salt.*

Love and eggs are best
when they are fresh.
　　　　　—*Russia*

Love and a cough cannot
be hidden.
　　　　　—*Latin*

Fear less, hope more; eat
less, chew more; whine
less, breathe more; talk
less, say more; hate less,
love more, and all good
things will be yours.
　　　　　—*Sweden*

A man in love mistakes a
harelip for a dimple.
　　　　　—*Japan*

In love, there is always
one who kisses and one
who offers the cheek.
　　　　　—*France*

It is easier to guard a
sack full of fleas than a
girl in love.
　　　　　—*Jewish*

A man in love schemes
more than a hundred
lawyers.
　　　　　—*Spain*

Loving a woman who
scorns you is like licking
honey from a thorn.
　　　　　—*Wales*

He Said

Who says men aren't chatty? These guys have plenty to say about women, wives, and love. See if you can match quote to speaker.

A. Oscar Wilde
B. Walt Disney
C. Brad Pitt
D. Albert Einstein
E. William M. Thackeray

F. Aristotle
G. Charlie Brown
H. Paul Newman
I. Steve Martin
J. Taye Diggs

1. "I like a woman with a head on her shoulders. I hate necks."
Hint: One wild and crazy guy

2. "Love is composed of a single soul inhabiting two bodies."
Hint: Philosopher whose works helped influence Western civilization

3. "I like to embarrass my wife. When we order Chinese food, sometimes I go to the door without my pants on. One time, the delivery guy just handed me my bag and ran."
Hint: Stage, film, and television actor best known for his role in the movie *How Stella Got Her Groove Back*

4. "Nothing takes the taste out of peanut butter quite like unrequited love."
Hint: Enjoys football, baseball, and kite flying

5. "Being married means I can break wind and eat ice cream in bed."
Hint: Academy Award nominee who got his start on TV shows like *Dallas*, *Growing Pains*, and *thirtysomething*

6. "Love is a better teacher than duty."
Hint: Smart guy

7. "Men always want to be a woman's first love—women like to be a man's last romance."
Hint: Witty Irish playwright

8. "I love Mickey Mouse more than any woman I've ever known."
Hint: (No hints for this one.)

9. "People stay married because they want to, not because the doors are locked."
Hint: Has the most famous eyes in Hollywood

10. "To love and win is the best thing. To love and lose, the next best."
Hint: British novelist who penned satires of high society

For answers, turn to page 176.

Unforgettable Proposals

*We've told you about public proposals (on page 47).
Now, take a look at some of the most unforgettable
and romantic proposals we could track down.*

eM yrraM

Proposer: Nick Lewis

Proposed: At a swimming party

Story: Scottish grammar school teachers Nick Lewis and
Lucy McKee were at a school party with their students, a
group of kids whose help Nick had enlisted for his proposal. Each child had a placard with a letter on it;
together the letters spelled "Miss McKee will you marry
Mr Lewis?" But when the time came for them to put their
letters together, the kids got it backward and spelled
"?siweL rM yrram uoy lliw eeKcM ssiM." (Hey—give 'em a
break—they were third graders!) It all worked out, though.
Lucy got the message . . . and said yes.

A Sentimental Man

Proposer: Blair Semple

Proposed: With a pipe cleaner

Story: As teenagers, Blair Semple and Phillippa Tully
were young and in love. They joked about getting married
one day; Blair even gave Phillippa a ring made from a pipe

cleaner. But as they grew up and went on with their lives, the jokes and the ring were put aside. They stayed in touch, though, continued to date, and eventually moved in together. Finally, after six years, Blair thought it was time to make good on the early promise. The couple took a walk on the beach with their dog, and after following a series of clues, Phillippa discovered that old pipe cleaner ring tied to the dog's collar. Blair then asked her to marry him, and she said yes (the pipe cleaner is now stored safely in their wedding album).

Pumpkins for Your Beloved

Proposer: Cameron McKergow
Proposed: Underwater
Story: Some guys bring flowers; Australian resident Cameron McKergow chose pumpkins. He called his girl-friend Julianne "pumpkin" as a term of endearment, so when he decided to ask her to marry him, it seemed log-ical to say it with fruit. Cameron planned a snorkeling trip to a bay in northern Australia, and after a few min-utes of floating around in the water, Julianne noticed a collection of pumpkins on the ocean floor. Closer inspection revealed that they were arranged to read "Marry me?" Julianne said yes, and it was a good thing, because the proposal had been a lot of work. While set-ting the scene, Cameron discovered that pumpkins float, and he had to weigh them all down with rocks to keep them underwater.

We've Come
a Long Way, Baby

*Since television's early days, programs have been pushing
the censors' limits. Here are some of the moments that
changed what we were allowed to see on TV.*

1947: Bedroom Antics

The first TV couple to share a bed was Mary Kay and
Johnny Stearns, married in real life and on the small
screen. Their show, *Mary Kay and Johnny*, ran from 1947
to 1950 and was also the first to
incorporate a real-life pregnancy into its story line;
in 1948, the Stearns' son
Christopher was writ-
ten in as a character.

1968: Kiss Me,
You Fool

Star Trek boldly went
where no man had gone
before and featured an
interracial kiss in 1968.

Captain Kirk (William Shatner) and Lieutenant Uhura (Nichelle Nichols) locked lips on the November 22 show, and several Southern stations protested, refusing to air the episode.

1972: Don't Ask, Don't Tell

The first gay character on TV was Peter Panama, played by Vincent Schiavelli on the short-lived 1972 series *The Corner Bar*. The character was dropped after the first season, but the show was canceled soon after anyway. The first well-known gay character on TV appeared in 1977 in the form of Jodie Dallas (Billy Crystal) on the hit show *Soap*. Many advertisers boycotted the show's early episodes but changed their minds when *Soap* became a hit.

1975: That's a Wrap

TV's first condom advertisement aired in 1975 on San Francisco's ABC affiliate, KNTV. The spot for Trojan lasted only 30 seconds but was quickly removed from the airwaves. Eleven years later, a television sitcom used the word "condom" in a story line for the first time. On the show *Valerie* (later renamed *The Hogan Family*), mom Valerie Hogan (Valerie Harper) mentioned condoms while trying to prepare her son David (Jason Bateman) for a date. Before the original broadcast of this episode, a parental advisory appeared.

1991: Abby and C.J. Sittin' in a Tree

Characters Abby and C.J. (Michele Greene and Amanda Donohoe) shocked *L.A. Law* viewers by sharing TV's first lesbian kiss on the February 7 episode. According to industry experts, the first French kiss between two gay men came more than 10 years later on an episode of *Dawson's Creek*. After breaking up with his girlfriend the previous season, Jack (Kerr Smith) smooched with boyfriend Ethan (Adam Kaufman) during the 2000 season finale.

Honorable Mention: Don't Flush!

It may not be love-related, but we couldn't pass up the opportunity to reveal the first toilet on television. In the early days of TV and through the 1970s, FCC regulations dictated that toilets not be shown on television—they were considered "indecent." But in 1957, the wholesome *Leave It to Beaver* managed to get around the censors by showing a toilet tank during the October 4 episode. The tank was allowed for two reasons: 1) it wasn't actually the whole toilet; just the tank, which was apparently more decent than the bowl; and 2) it was essential to the plot—Wally and the Beav bought a baby alligator from a mail order catalog and hid him in the toilet tank so their parents wouldn't find out.

Three percent of pet owners give their furry friends presents for Valentine's Day.

The Muse

*The original love goddess, she gave as good
as she got—if artistic results are any gauge.
What was it about Alma that made men wild?*

Raven-haired, quick-witted, and a talented musician, Alma Schindler moved in the highest artistic and intellectual circles in turn-of-the-century Vienna. Gustav Klimt, a friend of Alma's father and the painter of *The Kiss*, gave Alma her first kiss. But he wasn't the only artist she inspired.

Va-Va-Voom!

She was 22 when composer Gustav Mahler first saw her. He was 19 years older but smitten with her. Although flattered by his attention, Alma was torn—she was already having a passionate affair with her music tutor, Alexander Zemlinsky. But when Mahler (who eventually became conductor of the New York Metropolitan Opera) proposed a few weeks after their first meeting, she accepted. The two wed in 1902, making Zemlinsky the first in a long string of Alma's brokenhearted lovers.

Mahler supported his bride in fine style, and the couple had two daughters. During their years together, Mahler wrote five influential symphonies, but Alma was miserable. Mahler made her give up her own composing career, and he wouldn't let her go out on the town. She missed Vienna's lively social whirl.

How I Spent My Vacation

After eight unhappy years, Alma decided she needed a vacation. She took her daughter Anna to a spa resort where, somewhere between the mineral baths and the hotel rooms, Alma met a handsome German architect by the name of Walter Gropius (future founder of the Bauhaus school of design). The two embarked on a steamy affair during Alma's vacation, after which she took the train back to Vienna and her husband.

But Gropius wasn't ready to give her up, so he wrote a blistering love letter, which he mistakenly addressed to her husband. After reading Gropius's letter, Mahler had no peace. He sought help from Sigmund Freud, and the Mahlers experienced a brief second honeymoon. But it was too late—a genetic heart defect began to take its toll on Gustav. He died in 1911.

Alma cast her roving eye on Gropius, but he lost interest when he found out that Alma had slept with her husband right up until his death. But for Alma, there were plenty of other incredibly talented fish in the sea. Like painter Oskar Kokoschka. The press called him a wild, violent beast, and he was a social persona non grata. But the two began a three-year affair, during which it was said they stopped making love only long enough for Kokoschka to use Alma as a model for his paintings.

Kokoschka Goes Cuckooschka

Kokoschka was obsessed with Alma, but she remained a bit distant. This drove him so crazy that Kokoschka's mother threatened to shoot Alma dead if she came near her troubled son. Alma gave Kokoschka enough affection and sex to keep him interested, but she eventually tired of him and moved on. Kokoschka joined the military (at Alma's insistence) and fought in World War I.

With Kokoschka out of the picture, Alma took up with Gropius again. This time it took, at least for a while. They married in 1915. During their marriage, Gropius came to be known as one of the leading lights in European architecture.

When Kokoschka learned of their marriage, he had a life-size Alma doll made. Kokoschka walked the streets with his doll-friend, took it to parties and the opera, and used it as an artist's model. After some months, he gave a big party with champagne and music, exhibited the doll in a stunning costume, and when dawn came, he took it out to the garden, beheaded it, and broke a red wine bottle over it.

And Whose Baby Are You?

The real Alma had two children by Gropius, but in 1919 he learned that his third child had been fathered by someone else. Alma had met a young poet named Franz Werfel (who eventually wrote the novel *The Song of Bernadette*) two years earlier. They were mad for each other. They'd make love, and Alma would send him back to his writing desk the instant they'd finished, demanding that he improve his art to be worthy of her love. Gropius, defeated, agreed to a divorce.

In 1929, Alma and Werfel were married—she was 50, and he was 39. He started turning out a successful string of plays, poetry books, and novels. The two fled Austria for France just a few steps ahead of the Nazis (Werfel was Jewish). In Lourdes, Werfel made a vow that if he and Alma made a safe escape, he would write a book about St. Bernadette (which he did when the two immigrated to Hollywood in 1940).

Werfel died in 1945. Alma moved to New York and settled into a lavish apartment surrounded by her trophies: love letters, Mahler's scores, Kokoschka's paintings, and Werfel's manuscripts. She enjoyed the Manhattan social scene until her death in 1964. Though Alma herself only composed a few songs, she left a mark because, as she wrote in her autobiography, she held "for an instant the stirrups of her glorious knights."

Kissing for one minute burns 26 calories.

When Mom and Dad Pick 'Em

In India, 95 percent of marriages are arranged by someone other than the bridal couple. And in Japan, an estimated 25 percent of marriages are arranged. Although unpopular in most Western countries, arranged marriages are alive and well in the world today.

Some families employ matchmakers to find spouses for their children, but that's rare. Usually, parents do the choosing. Typically, parents begin by compiling a roster of suitable marriage candidates; some parents (particularly in India) also consult astrological charts to make sure a potential match is a good one. The criteria for choosing a match are based on class, education, wealth, and family connections, because the primary goal of making a good match is ensuring that the couple will be financially secure.

Catch Me a Catch!

Sometimes, parents let their children be involved in the process, though that depends on the family's values and traditions. The most conservative families leave every-thing up to Mom and Dad. Parents decide on the match without consulting their children, though they may reconsider if a child raises strenuous objections to a match. Often, in these cases, the couple doesn't meet for the first time until the wedding day.

Slightly more lenient parents suggest several choices and let their children choose a mate, though these parents are still the final arbiters.

More-modern parents allow their children to get to know each other before the wedding. Even so, the couple is seldom alone together. They are usually accompanied by a chaperone (often an older, married woman), who makes sure they aren't intimate before the nuptials.

And the most liberal arrangement is similar to blind dating. Parents provide their children with a list of acceptable marriage candidates, the child picks, and then the couple spends time getting together before deciding for themselves whether to wed.

Dowry Delights

In most places where arranged marriages are common, dowries remain the norm. These payments from a bride's family to a husband's can be in the form of money, clothes, jewelry, or even vacations. Here are some dowry facts (historical and modern) from around the world.

- In medieval Europe, it was considered charitable to pay a poor woman's dowry. In fact, the Christmas tradition of filling stockings with gifts may have arisen from the Turkish bishop Nicholas (later Saint Nicholas) throwing coins into the stockings of three poor sisters to serve as their dowries.

- Dowries represented one of the earliest recorded instances of state welfare system. During the Renaissance, one way the Italian government cared for orphaned girls was by paying their dowries when they were ready to marry.
- Today, in Sudan, men have to compete for a woman's hand. Tribesmen perform a dance in front of a prospective mate's family, trying to impress them with the height of their jumps. And Sudanese men have offered as many as 100 cows in exchange for a wife.
- In Korea, dowries historically involved appliances that would enable the newlyweds to set up house. Today, that tradition has gone high-tech. The most sought-after dowry gift in modern South Korea is a large-screen plasma TV.

In December 2005, a Massachusetts man found a diamond ring in his parked car. It came with a note that read "Merry Christmas. Thank you for leaving your car door unlocked. Instead of stealing your car, I gave you a present. Hopefully, this will land in the hands of someone you love, for my love is gone now." Police tried unsuccessfully to track down the person who left it behind.

Lovey-Dovey

You can't get more affectionate than these two love birds—they're filled with 33 romantic terms for you to snuggle up to. Awww!

AFFECTION	KISSES
AMOUR	LOVER'S LANE
ANGEL	LOVESICK
BABY	LOVE SONG
BILLET-DOUX	LUV
CHERUB	PARIS
CRUSH	ROMANCE
CUPCAKE	ROSES
DALLY	SERENADE
DOVE	SMACK
EMBRACE	SNOOKUMS
FLIRT	SWAK
GLANCE	SWEET NOTHINGS
HONEYBUN	SWEET TALK
HONEYMOON	TOOTSIE
HUGS	WOO
INFATUATION	

```
            F S N Q L         V E L E L
          T L W X O R       Y X D A I R
        C B O E V A K       S Q A L S T
          O P E Q E D L     N W N O T U
          T R T C V     M R O I E V O B
        T S B N R S         O N R E O Z A
      Y L Z A O F G         K F E S T V W
    X A B L M T V U L       U A S O A T V D
    N Q G A V H K H E       M T E N B K A Z
  E P D N Z B I O S G       S U K G F L P L N
  C B C Q V R N Q B N       Q A A R L T S O K
  X E H E W E G V L A       X T C Y I B E V A
  C L E M Y T S W A K       V I P A R I S E Q
  D X R B Q H Z D I B       O U M T L O S X
  H S U R C O X S F L       N C O W L R I F
    N B A W N S L S R       O U S E N C D
    B Z C X E M R Q         R D T O K
A W V T E S Y A F F E C T I O N P F D D S W K V
    L M S M C                 E O E
    Q X O K                   V U C
    T O V                     E P X
      N X E                   Q Z
        C D                   T
```

For answers, turn to page 178.

171

Quiz Answers

She Said, page 22

1. H – Hollywood costume designer Edith Head was nominated for 34 Academy Awards in her lifetime, more than any woman in history (she won eight times).

2. B – In addition to her successes on Broadway, Pearl Bailey served as a special ambassador to the United Nations, earned a theology degree from Georgetown University when she was 67, wrote several books, and was awarded the Presidential Medal of Freedom in 1988.

3. G – Many people consider Isadora Duncan to be the mother of modern dance. She pioneered the style during the late 19th and early 20th centuries, and, though she wasn't acclaimed in the United States during her lifetime, she was popular throughout Europe.

4. F – Lily Tomlin has found success in several entertainment genres. She's appeared in everything from Robert Altman's film *Nashville* (for which she earned an Oscar nomination) to the Broadway one-woman show *The Search for Signs of Intelligent Life in the Universe* (for which she won a Tony award) to TV's *The Magic School Bus* (for which she provided the voice of the teacher, Ms. Frizzle).

5. E – A vaudeville star who transitioned to a career in

Hollywood, Mae West made a name for herself by the time she was 12 years old, performing under the stage name "Little Vamp."

6. I – Rita Rudner married British writer Martin Bergman in 1989; three years later, the couple's first cowritten film (a comedy entitled *Peter's Friends*) made it to the big screen.

7. C – Agatha Christie's play *Mousetrap* holds the record for the longest-running stage play in London. *Mousetrap*'s opening night was November 25, 1952, and as of 2006, it had logged more than 20,000 performances.

8. J – In 1938, Katharine Hepburn lobbied producer David O. Selznick for the role of Scarlett O'Hara in *Gone with the Wind*. Selznick turned her down, saying she didn't have the sexual appeal necessary to play Scarlett. Instead, Vivien Leigh went on to play the woman who vowed never to go hungry again, and *Gone with the Wind* became the highest-grossing movie in film history (when adjusted for inflation).

9. A – In 2000, the *Guinness Book of World Records* called Madonna the world's most successful female recording artist; she's sold more than 200 million albums.

10. D – Helen Keller's mother, Kate, was inspired to find a way to educate her blind and deaf daughter after reading Charles Dickens's *American Notes*. In this book about his 1842 trip to North America, Dickens wrote about a blind and deaf woman named Laura Bridgman who had learned to read and speak while attending the Perkins School for the Blind in Massachusetts. Kate Keller wrote to the school, and 20-year-old Anne Sullivan was assigned to be Helen's teacher. Sullivan had learned several of the teaching techniques she used with Helen from Bridgman herself.

Down with Love, page 50

1. B – Nancy Sinatra's "These Boots Are Made for Walking" had an impact on many musicians who came after her. Madonna once said, "Nancy Sinatra was a huge influence on me. I wanted to put on my go-go boots and walk all over someone."

2. E – Gram Parsons's birth name was Ingram Cecil Connor III. He took the last name Parsons after his father died and his mother remarried a man named Bob Parsons. His first name, Gram, was short for Ingram.

3. F – Pete Yorn first gained mainstream success when his song "Strange Condition" appeared in the 2000 comedy *Me, Myself and Irene*.

4. D – No Doubt's Gwen Stefani began singing only because her older brother Eric pestered her into joining his band (Eric said she could sing and he couldn't, so it seemed a perfect fit). Their first song? "Stick It in the Hole," a tune about a pencil sharpener.

5. C – Before he became a star, the Police's Sting worked many odd jobs, including ditchdigger, milk delivery boy, and bus driver.

6. A – "Love Stinks" was the first real hit for the J. Geils

Band, but their 1981 tune "Centerfold" made them stars. That song stayed at number one for six weeks.

True Romance, Hollywood Style, page 75

1. D   2. B   3. F   4. G   5. A   6. C   7. E

"Love" on the Silver Screen, page 91

1. C   2. A   3. B   4. F   5. E   6. D

Make-Out Songs, page 134

1. B – Throat surgery in 1987 actually changed the tone of Elton John's voice. Before the surgery, he was known for singing in a falsetto, but afterward, he was no longer able to consistently achieve that sound.

2. C – Elvis Presley made "Can't Help Falling in Love" a hit, but numerous artists recorded it after him, from Perry Como to Anne Murray to Pearl Jam.

3. D – Frank Sinatra counted jazz singers Billie Holliday and Mabel Mercer among his most significant musical influences.

4. B – An Aerosmith-themed roller coaster (called the Rock 'n' Roller Coaster) opened at Florida's Walt Disney World in 1999. Riders climb into a stretch limousine–like car for the three-minute ride that reaches speeds of 60 mph and is the third-fastest ride at Disney World.

5. C – Whitney Houston is the only female artist to have two of the top 35 best-selling albums in the United States.

6. A – Marvin Gaye was born Marvin Pentz Gay in 1939.

He added the "e" to his last name in an effort to seem more professional.

7. B – In the early 1960s, rocker Rod Stewart had or tried out for several jobs. He tried out for a British soccer team, traveled Europe with a folk singing group, and worked as a grave digger.

8. C – The Beatles' first recording contract in 1962 paid them only one penny for every single sold in Great Britain and half a penny for every single sold outside of the country.

9. D – The character of Chef on *South Park* was modeled after Barry White, and *South Park*'s creators even offered him the job of voicing the character. White turned them down, however; as a devout Christian, he was offended by the show's content. Isaac Hayes took the part instead.

10. C – The original recording of "Love to Love You, Baby" that appears on the album of the same name is 17 minutes long.

He Said, page 156

1. I – One of Steve Martin's earliest jobs as a teenager was at Disneyland's Magic Shop.

2. F – Ancient Greek philosopher Aristotle studied and wrote about nearly every subject available in his time, from astronomy to zoology to politics to literature.

3. J – Actor Taye Diggs met his wife Idina Menzel (best known for originating the role of Elphaba in Broadway's *Wicked*), in 1996, when the two starred as Benny and

Maureen in the Tony award and Pulitzer prize–winning musical *Rent*.

4. G – Charlie Brown's unrequited love was the Little Red-Haired Girl, a character modeled after Donna Johnson, whom Peanuts creator Charles Schulz knew (and had a crush on) as a young man.

5. C – Brad Pitt attended the University of Missouri from 1981 to 1985. When he left school for Hollywood, he was just two credits away from earning a BA in journalism.

6. D – Albert Einstein was an early supporter of civil rights. He served as cochairman of the American Crusade to End Lynching (an anti-lynching organization founded in 1946 by actor and civil rights activist Paul Robeson) and once called racism "America's greatest disease."

7. A – More than a century after his death, Oscar Wilde remains a part of popular culture. Musicians (including Jimmy Buffet and the Smiths) have composed songs inspired by him, and references to Wilde have appeared in Monty Python skits, an episode of *Mystery Science Theater 3000*, and the 1998 film *Velvet Goldmine*.

8. B – Walt Disney met his wife, Lillian Bounds, in early 1925 when she took an administrative job at his fledgling studio (Disney Brothers Studio, run with his brother Roy Disney). The couple married a few months later on July 15.

9. H – Among Paul Newman's many Academy Award nominations (and one win for 1986's *Color of Money*) is one as producer for the film *Rachel, Rachel*, which starred his wife, Joanne Woodward (Woodward was also nominated for best actress, but neither won).

10. E – Although less frequently read today, in his time, William M. Thackeray was almost as popular as his contemporary Charles Dickens.

Lovey-Dovey, page 170

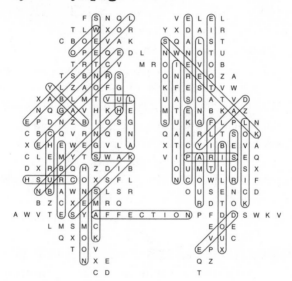